Journey to Jericho

Quilt Blocks and Symbols Inspired by the Bible

D0988828

by Kaye England
Text with Mary Elizabeth Johnson

Dedication

This book is dedicated to the wonderful men in my life. My life has been blessed by their presence. Their love, support and guidance in the past and present has made me believe in the future.

To those who have gone on ahead:

My devoted husband, David Rex England;

My beloved father, Robert Matthews Brown;

My dear brother, Robert Rex Brown.

To those who remain and enhance my life in some special way on a daily basis:

My incredible son, Bryan David England;

My adventuresome and enchanting grandsons, Austin David Richards and Nash Bryan England;

My delightful brother, David Ray Brown.

Page design and technique illustrations by Kevin Britton, Orlando, Florida.

Photography by Michael Negley, Los Angeles, California; Harold Kilgore, Birmingham, Alabama.; and Sid Rust, Indianapolis, Indiana.

Cover design by Janet Driscoll.

Printed in the USA.
Kaye England Publications
3137 E. Thompson Road
Indianapolis, Indiana 46227
www.quiltquarters.com or www.KayeEngland.com

ISBN: 0-9711168-1-4

Cover quilt: "Heirs of the Promise," by Lois D. Griffin, originally of Terre Haute, Indiana, now of Cave Creek, Arizona. See page 80 for more information.

Kaye England Publications
3137 East Thompson Road
Indianapolis, Indiana 46227
317-791-1336

www.KayeEngland.com

Table of Contents

Acknowledgments

I owe so many so much that I fear I'll overlook some names, so just know that I'm ever grateful to each of you. I must give a personal thanks to Mary Ellen Hopkins, my good friend, whose teachings and encouragement to grow have been invaluable. My first teaching seminar was with Mary Ellen and it has been a catalyst for my quilting life. Hopefully her zest and approach to quilting will be contagious. Thanks as well to David Hopkins, Mary Ellen's son, who published the first edition of this book.

My son and his wife, Bryan and Julie England, and my daughter, Sheila Richards, are a constant source of pride for me, and I love them dearly. I am especially thankful for my wonderful grandchildren—Chelsea Kaye, Morgan Taylor, Brylie Shea, Austin David, Nash Bryan, and Sydney Grace. Your Nana wishes you a life rich with happiness. (I believe grandchildren are our assurance that the prized quilts we produce will have a loving home awaiting them.)

Special thanks to quilters Harriet Hargrave, Cathy Franks, Leona Berg, Cecila Purciful, Stephanie Richardson and Alice Cunningham for all your beautiful work.

And to all of you, my hope is that this book will be as meaningful to you and your family as it is to me.

Kaye

The first and most significant person I want to thank is Kaye England, for allowing me to be a part of the revision of this book, which I know is very special to her. As it happens, she offered me the opportunity to work on the text just as I was experiencing a spiritual revitalization in my own life, so it has been doubly rewarding to delve into stories of the Bible and try to present them in such a way as to inspire a new perspective for you who will read them.

In the friendship I've shared with Kaye, it seems that she always gets to a place ahead of me, then turns around and pulls me to the new place. She made her mental journey to Africa ahead of me, then introduced me to its mystery and splendor, and "Quilt Inspirations from Africa" was the result. So it is with this book—although I've always known I wanted to do something with quilt blocks that are based on the Bible, Kaye did it ten years ahead of me. I'm so grateful that she turned around once again and brought me into another wonderful project.

Many of the people who work at St. John's Episcopal Church in downtown Montgomery, Alabama, of which I am a member, have been unfailingly helpful and supportive to me in this project. To them I offer my gratitude: The Rev. Mr. Robert C. Wisnewski, Jr., rector; The Rev. Mr. David Peeples and The Rev. Dr. James I. Walter, curates; Mrs. Lawrence Worrilow, office manager; and Mrs. Harry Allen, director of St. John's Flower Guild. I'd like also to thank my Thursday noon prayer group: Janet Hutto, Helen Wells, Betty Beale, and Rosa Davis. They regularly reaffirm for me that walking with God on a daily basis is a source of strength and happiness—one that I don't want to do without.

Mary Elizabeth

The Blocks and Their Stories

From Here to Jerusalem

Introduction

The inspiration for the name of the quilt and this quilt book is taken from the parable of the Good Samaritan. Jesus told this story in response to a question asked him by a lawyer, who began the conversation by asking Jesus how to get into heaven. Jesus tells him he should love his neighbor as himself, and the lawyer wants to know, "Who is my neighbor?"

And Jesus answering said, "*A certain man went down from Jerusalem to Jericho and fell among thieves which stripped him of his raiment, and wounded him, and departed, leaving him half-dead. And by chance there came down a certain priest that way and when he saw him, he passed by on the other side. And likewise, a Levite, when he was at that place, came and looked on him, and passed by on the other side. But a certain Samaritan, as he journeyed, came where he was; and when he saw him, he had compassion on him, and went to him, and bound up his wounds, pouring in oil and wine, and set him on his own beast, and brought him to an inn, and took care of him. And on the morrow when he departed, he took out two pence, and gave them to the host, and said unto him, 'Take care of him; and whatsoever thou spendest more, when I come again, I will repay thee.' Which now of these three, thinkest thou, was neighbor unto him that fell among thieves?" And He said, "He that showed mercy on him." Then said Jesus unto him, "Go, and do thou likewise.*" (**Luke 10:30-37**)

Many people have found this to be one of the most instructive of the stories (parables) Jesus used in his teaching. Not only is the unfortunate fellow robbed, beaten, stripped naked, and left for dead, he is ignored by a priest, of all people, and a temple assistant (the Levite). The wretchedness of their neglect is highlighted when, surprisingly, a Samaritan appears as the one who unselfishly cares for the victim, even up to spending two days' salary on him and promising more money if needed. The reason that Jesus chose a Samaritan to make his point was because the Samaritan would have been considered a social outcast, ceremoniously unclean, and a religious heretic from the Jewish point of view. The outcast, the person of no social stature, he who is the polar opposite of those who ignored the victim, proves to be a more caring and compassionate person than the priest and the temple assistant.

Beyond teaching us that we on earth are all brothers and sisters, Jesus shows us that we just never know who is going to turn out to be a good neighbor. And, as He makes clear, your neighbor is not just the person who lives next door to you.

We in the quilting realm have long known this last point to be true—our neighbors are all over the world. Even if another quilter doesn't speak the same language, communication is still possible through the shared love of fabric, pattern, color, and stitching. We are all neighbors, brought together by our love of the art of quilting. And, we are good neighbors—we all know, and can trust that, each of us stands ready to help any other of us in any way possible. That is the most satisfying and enriching aspect of being a quilter, and it surpasses any skill you may attain.

There Are Many Versions of the Bible

It is entirely possible that everyone who buys this book reads a different Bible! There are many translations and versions of the Book, so it may be that the verses we highlight on these pages differ slightly from what you will find in your own personal Bible. Kaye uses the King James Version; Mary Elizabeth uses the Revised English Bible from the Oxford University Press and the Revised Standard Version, from Thomas Nelson & Sons. Although the last two versions may be a bit easier to understand, there's no substitute for the poetry and beauty of language in the King James Version.

Each of us relied heavily on commentaries in preparing the text that accompanies the twelve different blocks and the quilting designs. We are very much like the Ethiopian official in this passage from **Acts 8:30-31**: *"So Philip ran to him and heard him reading Isaiah the prophet, and asked, 'Do you understand what you are reading?' And he said, 'How can I, unless someone guides me?'"* Even centuries ago, when they were nearer in time to the events that they were reading about, readers found some of the books of the Bible difficult to truly know without learned help.

One reason for this is that the Bible is a compilation of books written originally in three different languages: Hebrew, Aramaic (the language of Persia), and Greek. Each person who translated the books into their own language, from which we have eventually translated our English versions, has had to make a judgment on what particular words mean. It is said that "translation is interpretation," and that is why there are still so many different points of view about what certain, especially those particularly confusing, parts of the Bible really mean.

Fortunately, most of the blocks in this book are symbolic of an historical event, rather than of a theological point that is difficult to illustrate. You will have your own personal reasons for making a quilt based on the Bible, and you will have your own interpretations of the meanings of the blocks, and the Bible verses, and the stories. And, in the end, it is your interpretation that is the most important, because that is what determines the significance of the quilt to you and your loved ones.

How to Plan a Meaningful Quilt

The Bible has greatly influenced quiltmakers for at least two centuries, and there are a multitude of different blocks named for stories, objects, and incidents in both the Old and New Testaments. However, with some thought and planning, your quilt can impart even more meaning than is apparent from the name of the block, as you will see.

The twelve blocks featured in the quilt and in this book were chosen either because the design was especially appealing, or because the stories they represented were so rich with meaning. The blocks are arranged so that they follow the same order of appearance as do their sources of inspiration in the Bible—Old Testament blocks first, then New Testament.

The size of each block is eight inches, for two reasons. One is that many of the other sources on this subject presented blocks that were either ten or twelve inches, and a smaller size would give a fresh perspective for this publication. Also, eight is the number of the Resurrection, for it was on the eighth day after His entry into Jerusalem that Christ rose from the grave.

Three of the blocks seemed to be particularly suited for medallion-style quilts—"Tree of Life," "Joseph's Coat," and "Bethlehem Star." Therefore, templates and cutting directions are given for sixteen-inch blocks of these three patterns only.

Twelve, the number of pieced blocks in the quilt, has always been a favorite number in Christian symbolism. It is the number of Apostles and is occasionally used to represent the entire Church.

There are six setting blocks, six being the number of creation and perfection. These symbolize divine power, majesty, wisdom, love, mercy, and justice.

There are ten side blocks, the number of the Ten Commandments. The four corner blocks represent the four evangelists, Matthew, Mark, Luke, and John.

Three was called by Pythagorus the number of completion, expressive of a beginning, a middle, and an end. In Christian symbolism, three became the divine number, suggesting the Trinity and also the three days between Jesus' death and resurrection. This number could also be symbolic of the completed quilt: the top, a beginning; the batting, the middle; and the backing, an end!

Color Symbolism

The colors you choose for your quilt can add greatly to its depth of meaning. Although color symbolism is an area where there are no clear and fast rules, there are some generally accepted notions of what different colors represent; however, the intriguing thing about nearly all symbols is that they often express both the positive and the negative sides of a concept. For example, if a color stands for joy, it can also stand for sorrow. The important thing is that you know what you were planning to express through your color choices. The following list presents the most generally accepted meanings of certain colors in the Christian sense.

Purple/Violet (the terms are used interchangeably) is associated with royalty. It is the sign of imperial power, and is often used as a symbol of God the Father. It can also be the color of sorrow, suffering, penitence, and expectation; on the other hand, it can represent love, truth, and the Passion. Purple is the liturgical color for Lent and Advent. It is an excellent choice for the background of the cover quilt, and by extension, the cover of this book, because it stands for the feelings most of us want to express when we do a quilt based on the Bible.

Blue symbolizes heaven and heavenly love. It is also recognized as the color of truth, because the sky always appears blue after a storm, implying that the clouds, which obscure reality, have been cleared away. Some churches use a deep indigo blue during Advent, rather than purple.

Green is the color of spring and new vegetation, symbolizing the triumph of seedtime over winter, life over death. It is the color for Epiphany and Pentecost.

Red, because it is the color of blood and of fire, is associated with the emotions, and represents both love and hate. It may be used instead of purple during Holy Week—Palm Sunday through Holy Saturday. Red is used on certain Holy Days throughout the year: Pentecost (Whitsunday); all feast days for the apostles and the evangelists; for Holy Cross Day, Saint Stephen, the Holy Innocents, and Saint James of Jerusalem.

Yellow also has a twofold meaning. Golden yellow symbolizes the sun and divinity. On the other hand, yellow also suggests jealousy, treason, and deceit.

The colors that quilters regard as neutrals—black, gray, brown, and white—have, unfortunately, mostly negative connotations. In most Bible-based quilts, these colors will serve the same purpose as they do in quilts that do not have a religious theme—that of providing a background for the other colors in the design. However, there may be occasions when a quilter wishes to use these colors to represent meaningful events in their lives and will be grateful for the emotions and events they symbolize.

Brown signifies spiritual death and degradation and renunciation of the world.

Black is a symbol of deep mourning, and may be used as a liturgical color on Good Friday.

Gray is the color of ashes, thereby expressing mourning and humility.

White is the neutral that has no negative associations; it is the symbol of innocence, purity, and holiness. White is the liturgical color for Easter and Christmas, and certain other Holy Days throughout the year: Epiphany Sunday; The First Sunday after the Epiphany; Trinity Sunday; The Holy Name; the Presentation; the Annunciation; The Visitation; Saint John the Baptist; The Transfiguration; Saint Joseph; Saint Mary Magdalene; Saint Mary the Virgin; Saint Michael and All Angels; All Saints Day. White is the color used in the church during the national holidays of Independence Day and Thanksgiving Day.

Summary

The ancient place, Jericho, was an oasis, one of the green spots in the desert north of the Dead Sea, in the Rift Valley. It was a destination for the trading caravans that criss-crossed Palestine in Biblical times. An oasis a little further to the south, En-gedi, was famed for its beauty and fertility, with "henna flowers among the vines" (Song of Solomon 1:14). There is no reason to think that Jericho was not equally beautiful.

The original meaning of the word "Jerusalem" is "possession of peace;" that of Jericho, "a place of fragrance." Who among us would refuse a journey that went between two equally delightful places - from one of peace to one of fragrance?

As you begin your journey to Jericho, may it be a fulfilling and enjoyable trip. We have learned much along the road.

Lord, my heart is not haughty, nor mine eyes lofty: neither do I exercise myself in great matters, or in things too high for me .
Psalms 131:1

Tree of Life

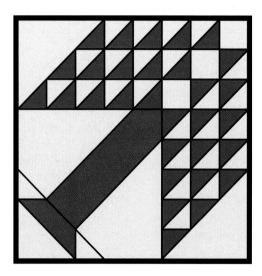

Trees have had symbolic significance for all civilizations since the beginning of history. In the Bible, they are a symbol of plenty, goodness, wisdom, and the ideal relationship of work and trust between man and God. "*And the Lord God planted a garden eastward in Eden; and there He put the man whom he had formed. And out of the ground made the Lord God to grow every tree that is pleasant to the sight and good for food; the Tree of Life also in the midst of the garden, and the Tree of Knowledge of good and evil.*" (**Genesis 2:8-10**).

(It was the fruit of the Tree of Knowledge with which the serpent tempted Eve; the resulting series of events is well-known to all who attended Sunday School. There is a legend that after the death of Adam, the Archangel Michael instructed Eve to plant a branch of the Tree of Knowledge on his grave. From this branch grew a tree which Solomon moved to his temple's garden. Later, the tree was uprooted and thrown into the pool of Bethesda, where it remained until it was taken out to be made into the cross on which Jesus was crucified.)

The Tree of Life has always been intriguing to students of the Bible. Some writers held the opinion that this Tree had secret virtues, and could somehow preserve or extend life. A philosopher of the first century, Philo Judeus, was the first of many theologians to believe that the story of creation was a divine allegory, in which the Tree of Life was a symbol of religion. A brilliant third-century theologian, Origen, also believed that the story of the creation was a metaphor, in which trees represented angels, Eden was heaven, and rivers of the world were wisdom. That it is an instructive story is beyond doubt; every great civilization of the ancient world had a tale of how the earth and humanity came into being. There are a number of surprising similarities between the one in the Bible and those of other religions.

In **Proverbs 3:18**, wisdom is compared to the Tree of Life: "*She is a Tree of Life to them that hold upon her; and happy is everyone that retaineth her.*"

The Tree of Life spoken of in **The Revelation to St. John** is an emblem of the joys of the celestial paradise. "*He that hath an ear, let him hear what the spirit saith unto the Churches; to him that overcometh will I give to eat of the Tree of Life which is in the midst of the paradise of God.*" (the **Revelation to St. John 2:7**), and "*On either side of the river stood a Tree of Life, which yields twelve crops of fruits, one for each month of the year; and the leaves of the Tree were for the healing of the nations*" (**Revelation 22:2**). And a few verses later, in the **Revelation 22:14**, "*Blessed are they that do His commandments, that they may have right to the Tree of Life, and may enter in through the gates into the city.*"

From the first book of the Bible to the last, the Tree of Life plays an important part in Christian symbolism.

Quick-Piecing Half-Square Triangles

Use this quick-piecing technique for the easiest way to make a basketful of Half-Square triangle units! Visit your local quilt store to find preprinted Half-Square triangle paper, or make your own. The instructions that follow are for marking directly on the fabric. Marked lines will become the cutting lines for your units.

1. Determine finished size of your triangles and add ⅞". This will set the size of your drawn squares.

2. Mark grids on back of the lightest fabric (arrows indicate size determined in step 1).

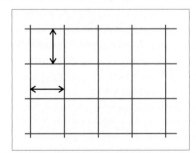

3. Beginning at the upper left square, mark a line from upper right (a) to lower left (g), skip a square then mark another line from point (b) to (f) and from point (c) to (e).

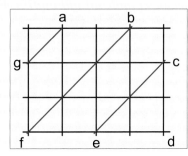

4. Repeat this process starting at upper right-hand square (b to c), (a to d) and (g to e).

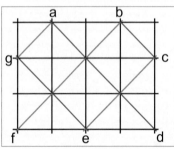

5. Lay marked fabric onto second fabric, rightsides together and pin as indicated by the red dots on the drawing below.

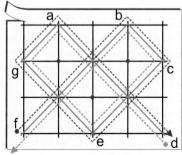

6. Starting at lower left (see red dot at "f"), sew ¼" from marked line all the way around the grid to "d" (red line).

7. Repeat on other side of lines (see blue line beginning at "d," finishing at "f").

8. Cut on all solid marked lines (horizontal, vertical and diagonal).

In this example, you'll get 24 finished half-square triangle units! Trim to size needed.

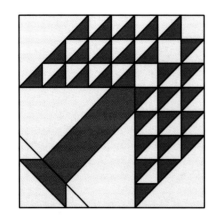

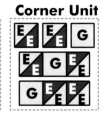

Leaf-1 Unit   Corner Unit

Trunk Unit   Leaf-2 Unit

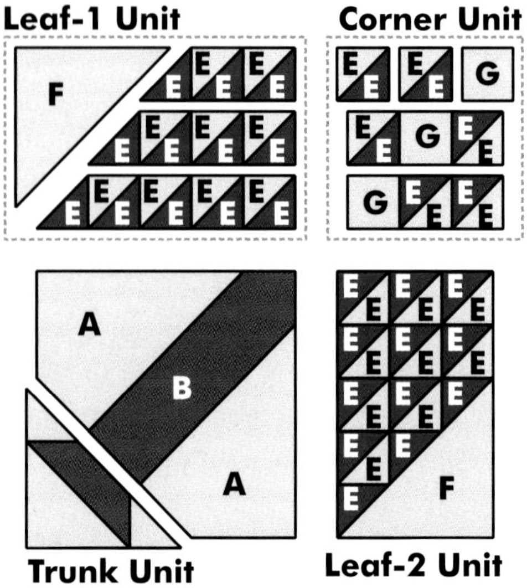

Cut the following to make one block:

Fabric	Template	Cut	Yield	8"	16"	Instructions
Light	A	1	2	5c"	10c"	Square, Cut diagonally into half-square triangles
Dark	B	1	-	1⅞ x 7¾	2⅞ x 14¾	Strip
Light	C	1	-	2⅞"	4⅞"	Square, Cut diagonally into half-square triangles
Dark	C	1	-	2⅞"	4⅞"	Square, Cut diagonally into half-square triangles
Light	D	2	-	1½ x 2½"	2½ x 4½"	Rectangles
Light	E	12	24	1⅞"	2⅞"	Squares, Cut diagonally into half-square triangles
Medium	E	15	30	1⅞"	2⅞"	Squares, Cut diagonally into half-square triangles
Light	F	1	2	3⅞"	6⅞"	Squares, Cut diagonally into half-square triangles
Light	G	3	-	1½"	2½"	Squares

Tree of Life (finishes 8" or 16")

Ease construction of this seemingly daunting block by breaking it into four "units". Use appropriate measurements for the size block that you choose to make, 8" or 16".

1. Following the diagrams at right, make the "trunk" unit. (See next page for constuction using templates.)

    a. Fold the pieces (A) and (B) in half (see "center line" marking on illustration), finger-press and sew together matching the creased lines. Trim the unit to 5½" square.

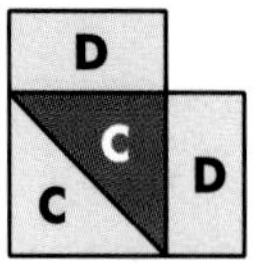

    b. Sew the light and dark half-square triangles (C) together.

    c. To adjacent sides of the dark triangle attach the light strips (D) to make the "base" unit.

    d. Position "base" unit on the "trunk" unit as illustrated (right sides together and the "hole" at the bottom corner). Stitch diagonally through as if it were a connector square (see page 45 for details).

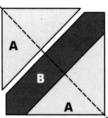

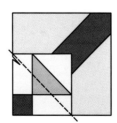

    e. Trim away excess "base," press back to complete unit.

2. Following the "leaf-1" diagram, connect the dark and light half-square triangle pieces* (E) together; note the unsewn triangles (E) are sewn to the end of the rows for the larger units. Complete the unit by attaching corner piece (F).

3. Make "Leaf-2" unit in the same manner; note arrangement of pieces is the reverse of "Leaf-1" unit.

4. The small "Corner" unit is made of dark and light half-square triangle pieces (E) and light squares (G). Use the diagram for placement of pieces.

5. Sew the four units together into a large square.

* Use the "quick piecing" technique to make a large number of the half-square triangle units quickly and accurately. See previous page for details.

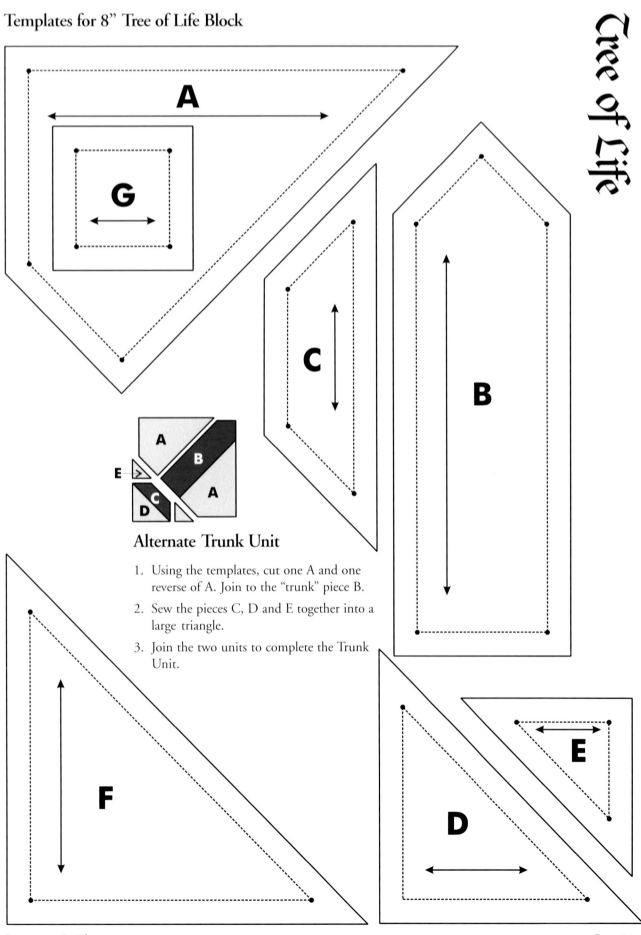

Tree of Life

A

G

C

B

Alternate Trunk Unit

1. Using the templates, cut one A and one reverse of A. Join to the "trunk" piece B.

2. Sew the pieces C, D and E together into a large triangle.

3. Join the two units to complete the Trunk Unit.

F

E

D

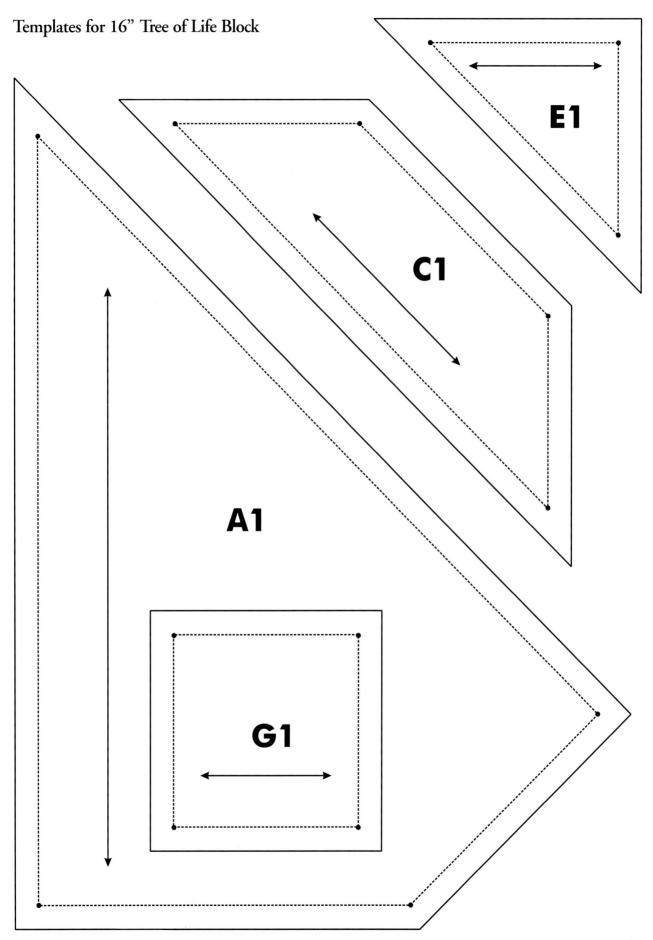

E1

C1

A1

G1

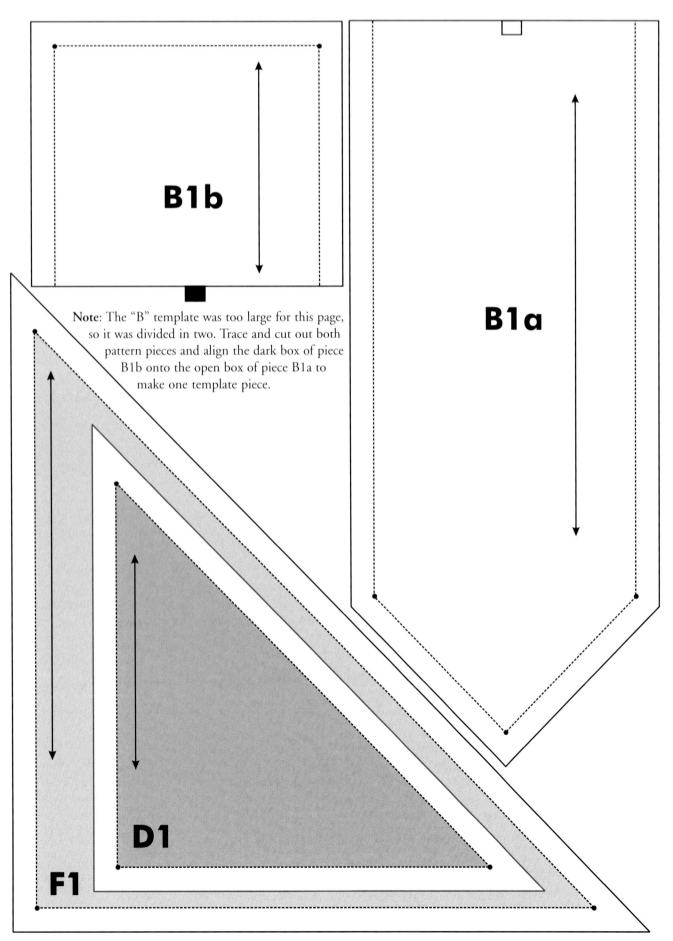

B1b

Note: The "B" template was too large for this page, so it was divided in two. Trace and cut out both pattern pieces and align the dark box of piece B1b onto the open box of piece B1a to make one template piece.

B1a

D1

F1

Jacob's Ladder

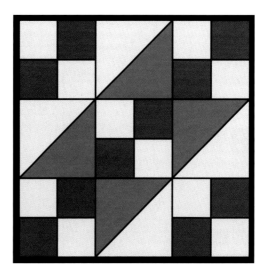

According to **Genesis 25:23**, the rivalry between Jacob and Esau, Isaac's twin sons, was foretold before they were born. During her difficult pregnancy, Rebekah went to a holy place to consult with God and was told, *"There are two nations in your womb: your issue will be two rival peoples. One nation will have the mastery of the other, and the elder will serve the younger."*

As the children grew, they proved to be of entirely different temperaments—Esau loved the outdoors and was a great hunter of wild game and became his father's favorite; Jacob, however preferred the pleasures of the hearth, which endeared him to his mother. Perhaps because of his father's inclination toward Esau, Jacob employed devious methods to get himself a share of his father's gifts: once, Jacob demanded Esau's birthright before giving him a bowl of soup; on another occasion, Jacob fooled his father into giving him the blessing that should have been Esau's.

"Now he has supplanted me twice. First he took my birthright and now he has taken my blessing," Esau cried, vowing to kill Jacob as soon as Isaac was dead (**Genesis 27:36, 41**). Rebekah, fearing for Jacob's life, sent him to live with her brother. On the way to his uncle's house, Jacob stopped for the night at a religious shrine.

"He took one of the stones there and, using it as a pillow under his head, he lay down to sleep. In a dream he saw a ladder, which rested on the ground with its top reaching to heaven, and angels of God were going up and down on it. The Lord was standing beside him saying, 'I am the Lord, the God of your father Abraham and the God of Isaac. This land on which you are lying I shall give to you and your descendants. They will be countless as the specks of dust on the ground, and you will spread far and wide, to west and east, to north and south. All the families of the earth will wish to be blessed as you and your descendants. . .'" (**Genesis 28:11-18**).

Jacob made his way on to his uncle's house, where he was accepted as a member of the family. He married sisters, Leah and Rachel, and had ten sons by Leah and the two slave-girls that came with the sisters as dowry; Rachel, barren for many years, eventually gave birth to Joseph. After twenty years in a foreign land, Jacob set out to return home.

Somewhat apprehensive about how Esau would accept his return, Jacob decided to ensure his welcome by sending a party ahead with a lavish gift of goats, cows, camels and donkeys. He sent his family and all that he had behind the drovers of the gift herd, and stayed alone in the desert that night. "A *man wrestled with him there until daybreak. When the man saw that he could not get the better of Jacob, he struck him in the hollow of his thigh, so that Jacob's hip was dislocated as they wrestled. The man said, 'Let me go, for day is breaking,' but Jacob replied, 'I will not let you go unless you bless me.' The man asked, 'What is your name?' 'Jacob,' he answered. The man said, "Your name shall no longer be called Jacob, but Israel, because you have striven with God and with mortals and have prevailed'"* (**Genesis 32:23-28**).

Jacob then looked up and saw Esau coming with four hundred men; as he went to meet him, Jacob bowed low to the ground seven times as he approached his brother. Esau ran forward and embraced him; he threw his arms round him and kissed him, and they both wept (**Genesis 33:3-40**).

From that day forward the brothers lived as family, although Jacob cautiously chose to live a distance away from Esau, buying property from relatives. When their father, Isaac, died at age 180, the brothers joined together to bury him. However, in fulfillment of the original prophecy about warring twins that Rebekah was given, genuinely peaceful relations were not to be for the brothers' offspring. Joseph's descendants became the nation of Israel; Esau's, the kingdom of Edom, and there are repeated references in the Old Testament to the two kingdoms struggling against one another; most often, apparently, Edom was trying to gain independence from Israel.

Connector Corner Flying Geese

Make quick work of this unit by using Connector Corners!

1. Determine finished size of triangle needed (the height of the rectangle).

2. Add ⅞" to that measurement.

3. Cut the square(s) to this size.

4. Lay the Connector square onto the base fabric right sides together.

5. Mark a diagonal line through square as illustrated.

6. Sew along the line.

7. Trim the excess fabric leaving ¼" seam allowance (do not cut the base fabric).

8. Press the fabric onto itself to form the corner triangle.

9. Repeat for other side of unit.

Jacob's Ladder

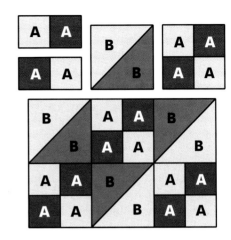

Cut the following to make one block:

Fabric	Template	Cut	Yield	Instructions
Light	A	10	-	Template A
Dark	A	10	-	Template A
Light	B	4	-	Template B
Medium	B	4	-	Template B

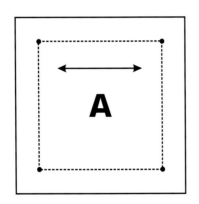

Jacob's Ladder (finishes 8")

1. Using the technique described in "Hints and Tips," page 67, and the templates at right, cut out all the pieces needed for the block.

2. Sew light and dark squares (A) together into a 4-patch squares. Make five.

3. Join the light and medium triangles (B) together into pairs. Make four.

4. Following the diagram at top of page, sew the units above into alternating strips.

5. Sew strips together to complete block.

Although this is a simple block, the odd measurements indicate the use of templates will give you more accurate results.

Quick Half-Square Triangles

1. Determine finished size of triangle needed.

2. Add ⅞".

3. From both fabrics, cut a square to this measurement.

4. With squares placed right-sides together, mark a diagonal line on the back of the lighter square.

5. Sew ¼" on each side of the line.

6. Cut on the marked line.

7. Press the units open to yield two half-square triangle units!

The elder of two sons of Jacob by his beloved Rachel, Joseph was about six years old when his father returned to Canaan and took up residence in the town of Hebron. It was at this point in Jacob's life that God gave him his new name—he would thenceforth be called Israel. (See **Genesis 35:10.**)

The fine coat that Israel gave to Joseph is described in different ways in the many translations and versions of the Bible. All versions agree that Joseph was Israel's favorite son; we can be assured that the coat was a special gift and as grand as could be procured. "*Now Israel loved Joseph more than all his children, because he was the son of his old age; and he made him a coat of many colors*" (**Genesis 37:3**). "*He made him a long robe with sleeves,*" says another translation, which may be interpreted to mean a garment long and full, such as was worn by the children of the ruling class. The original phrase may, however, also be rendered as "a coat of many pieces," or, as we quilters like to think, a patchwork incorporating myriad colors.

By the time Joseph reached about seventeen years of age, he had incurred the dislike of his brothers. They "*hated him and could not speak peaceably unto him. Their anger was increased when he told them of his dreams*" (**Genesis 37:4-5**). Eventually, in a fit of jealous rage, the brothers sold Joseph for twenty pieces of silver to Ishmaelite caravaners traveling through Canaan to Egypt. To cover up their hateful act, the brothers took Joseph's special coat and dipped it in the blood of a goat, then told their father they had found the blood-stained coat in a pit. Israel, believing a beast had devoured his favorite son, was inconsolable in his grief.

While his father mourned for him, Joseph's fortunes were, surprisingly, steadily rising. (*Joseph prospered, for the Lord was with him* - **Genesis 39:2**.) Not long after the Ishmaelites sold him to Potiphar, a captain of the guard in Pharaoh's army, Joseph was recognized as a person of honesty and diligence and put in charge of managing Potiphar's estates.

However, it was Joseph's ability to interpet dreams, one of the things about him most despised by his brothers, that was ultimately responsible for his extraordinary career. When Pharaoh had a puzzling dream of seven fat cows that were eaten up by seven lean cows, Joseph was the only person in Egypt who coluld explain what the dream meant. Egypt would have seven years of abundance, Joseph said, which would be followed by seven years of drought. He further advised Pharaoh to prepare during the years of plenty for the years of famine. Recognizing his wisdom, Pharaoh appointed Joseph to the highest position in the land, second only to himself.

As the years passed, all the lands adjoining Egypt were affected by the famine, and the word went out that there was food for man and beast only in Egypt. Suffering the deprivation as others were, Israel decided to send his sons into Egypt to obtain food for his family. During the trading that subsequently took place, the Canaanites had no idea that the Egyptian official they dealt with was their brother. Although Joseph immediately recognized them, he did not let them know. After posing a number of tests to his brothers to learn as much as possible about the current situation with his family, and to verify the brothers' current state of integrity, Joseph finally revealed himself to his family and gathered them all into Egypt, so that he could tend to them.

All the brothers came, with their children and grandchildren, led by Israel. The family numbered 70 when it entered Egypt. *Israel sent Judah ahead to Joseph to advise him that he was on his way to Goshen. They entered Goshen, and Joseph had his chariot yoked to go up there to meet Israel his father. When they met, Joseph threw his arms round him and wept on his shoulder for a long time* (**Genesis 46:29**). Israel said to Joseph, "*I have seen for myself that you are still alive. Now I am ready to die*" (**Genesis 46:30**).

Templates for 8" Joseph's Coat Block

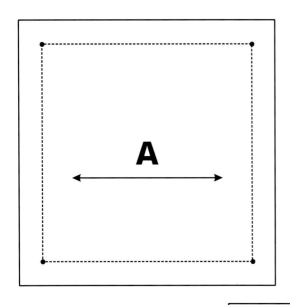
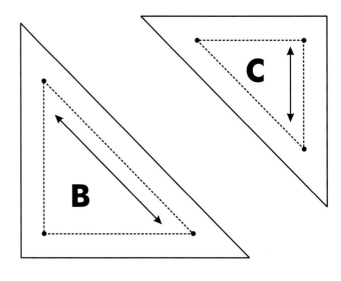
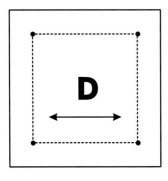
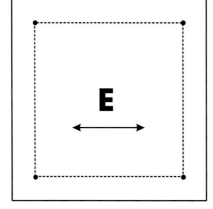
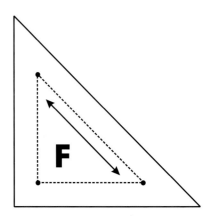

Cut the following to make one block:

Fabric	Template	Cut	Yield	Instructions
Dark1	A	1	-	Template A (16" - A1)
Medium1	B	16	-	Template B (16" - B1)
Dark2	C	16	-	Template C (16" - C1)
Medium2	C	16	-	Template C (16" - C1)
Light	D	4	-	Template D (16" - D1)
Dark1	E	4	-	Template E (16" - E1)
Light	F	4	-	Template F (16" - F1)

Joseph's Coat (finishes 8" or 16")

This block breaks into the center square and four identical corner units. Be sure to choose templates for the size block you want to make.

1. Make the center unit first.

   a. Make the four Flying Geese units with medium1 (B) and dark2 (C) pieces.

   b. Sew two of the Flying Geese units to opposite sides of the dark1 center square (A).

   c. Attach the light squares (D) to each end of the remaining two Flying Geese units.

   d. Sew these strips to top and bottom of center unit

2. Assemble four of the corner units.

   a. Attach the medium2 pieces (C) to each side of the dark1 pieces (E).

   b. Sew the medium1 triangles (B) to three adjacent sides of the corner units.

   c. Join the light triangles (C) to opposite sides of the unit to "square off."

3. Sew two of the corner units to opposite sides of the center unit.

4. To the remaining two corner units, add the light "wings" (F) to opposite sides.

5. Attach the final two corner units to opposite sides to complete block.

Templates for 16" Joseph's Coat Block

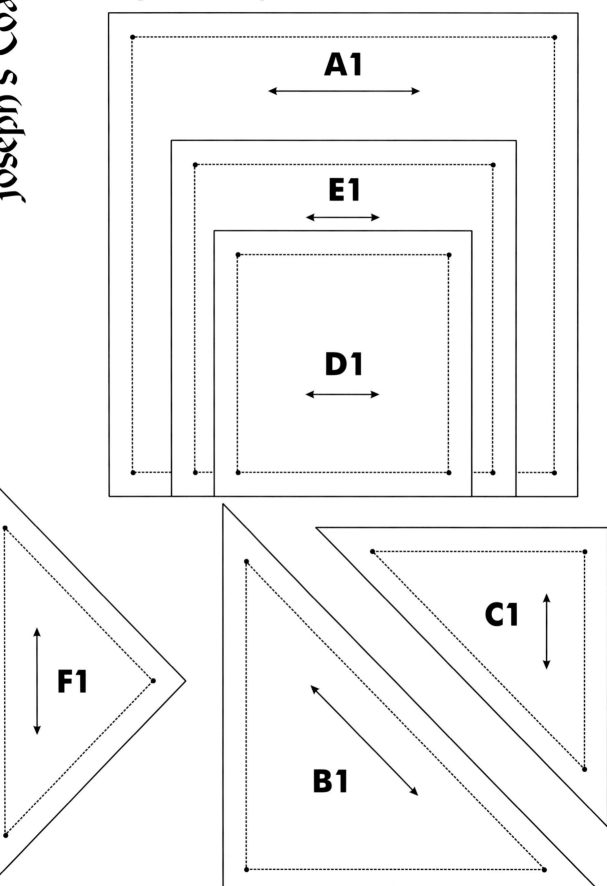

David (the name means "beloved"), was the eighth and youngest son of Jesse, a modest citizen of Bethlehem; David's mother's name is not recorded. (Some scholars think she was the Nahash of **II Samuel 17:25**.) As to David's personal appearance, we know that he was "*red haired, with beautiful eyes and goodly to look at.*" Or, in another translation, "*handsome, with ruddy cheeks and bright eyes*" (**I Samuel 16:12**).

Goliath (translates as "great," meaning "large;" he was either nine or ten feet tall), was probably a descendant of the Rephaim, who found refuge among the Philistines after they were dispersed by the Ammonites (**Deuteronomy 2:20:21**). Goliath's appearance and military equipment are described in more detail than any other soldier in the Bible.

The Philistines and Israelites were traditional enemies, and in one of the on-going battles fought between the two tribes, Goliath taunted his opponents by striding each day for forty days—nearly six weeks!—to the front of his army, demanding an Israeli champion to fight. The Israelites were thrown into a panic, because they figured they had no one to match the size and strength of this Philistine giant.

Much of the rest of the story is familiar; David, the simple shepherd boy who had been sent to the battlefront by his father to learn how his brothers were faring, volunteered to be Israel's champion. Refusing any armor for protection, because he found it uncomfortable, little David picked up some stones from the riverbed and, armed only with his sling and shepherd's staff, walked toward the giant.

Goliath was insulted that a person of such boyish appearance, with such simple weapons, should dare approach him. He spoke to David, "*Am I a carrion dog, that thou comest out against me with naught but a staff in thy hand? Come to me, and I will give thy flesh unto the fowl of the air, and to the beasts of the fields*" (**I Samuel 17:43**).

David and Goliath

The Philistine and Israelite armies faced each other from opposing hillsides, with a valley between. As they advanced toward one another in the valley, David, staying cautiously beyond the reach of a javelin throw, circled about Goliath, causing the giant to turn and, ultimately, face the blazing sun. As David maneuvered his opponent into position, he called across the stillness to Goliath.

"Thou hast come out against me, armed with sword and spear and javelin. A brazen shield is on thine arm and thou art hung head to foot with armor of brass. But if this be all thy strength, beware of it! For I am come out against thee in the name of the Lord of Hosts, the God of the armies of Israel, whom thou hast insulted and defied, and this day the Lord will deliver thee into my hand. And I will smite thee. That all the earth may know there is a God in Israel, and that His salvation is not in sword and spear, not His battle to the strong, but that He giveth victory according as He decree." (**I Samuel 17:45-47**).

Then, before Goliath could strike a single blow, David ran rapidly towards the giant, whirling his sling above his head, his gaze fixed gravely on his huge target. Then David lifted his thumb and set the stone sailing through the air. It hit the Philistine in the middle of his forehead, and, without so much as a groan, the giant fell face down upon the ground. (Some accounts say the stone actually entered Goliath's head!) David took Goliath's own sword and cut the giant's head off. Seeing their champion slain, the Philistines fled. David strode off the field of battle, carrying Goliath's head and his sword. The sword was later preserved as a religious trophy at a temple in the village of Nob (**I Samuel 21:1-9**).

The reigning king of Israel, Saul, took David permanently into his household after the victory. David's life of extraordinary adventure and service to God was only beginning when he battled Goliath. (See "King David's Crown," page 24, for more about David's life.)

Templates for David and Goliath Block

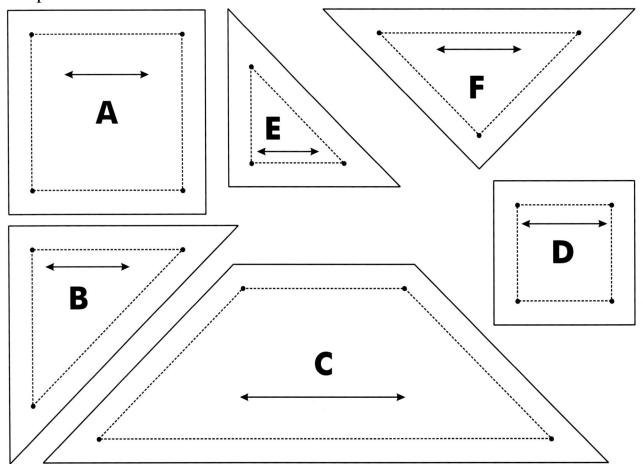

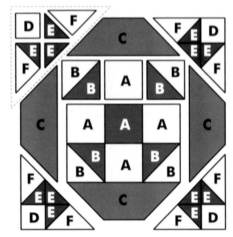

Cut the following to make one block:

Fabric	Template	Cut	Yield	Instructions
Dark1	A	1		2⅛" Square
Light	A	4		2⅛" Squares
Dark1	B	2	4	2½" Squares, Cut diagonally into half-square triangles
Light	B	2	4	2½" Squares, Cut diagonally into half-square triangles
Medium	C	1	4	6⅛" Square, Cut twice diagonally into quarter-square triangles
Light	D	4		1½" Squares
Dark2	E	6	12	1⅞" Squares, Cut diagonally into half-square triangles
Light triangles	F	2	8	3¼" Squares, Cut twice diagonally into quarter-square

David & Goliath Block (finishes 8")

1. Sew the light and dark1 half-square triangles (B) together into pairs.

2. Following the diagram for color placement, sew the half-square triangle units and the light and dark squares (A) together into a checkboard square.

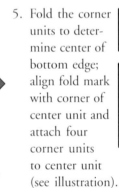

3. Sew the four quarter-square triangles (C) to the sides of the center unit. Do not trim yet.

4. Assemble the four corners.

   a. Sew the light square (D) to one of the dark half-square triangles (E)

   b. Attach a light quarter-square triangle (F) to right side of half-square triangle (E) to make a row.

   c. Sew a light quarter-square triangle (F) to half-square triangle (E).

   d. Finish second half of unit by attaching the dark half-square triangle (E) to right edge of the dark half-square triangle (see illustration at right).

   e. Sew the two units together into a larger triangle.

   f. Trim the excess edge of the (F) triangle.

5. Fold the corner units to determine center of bottom edge; align fold mark with corner of center unit and attach four corner units to center unit (see illustration).

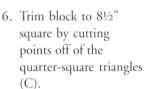

6. Trim block to 8½" square by cutting points off of the quarter-square triangles (C).

King David's Crown

A consequence of David's heroic deed in killing the giant Goliath (page 21-23) was that a jealousy was awakened in King Saul (**I Samuel 18:6-16**), although things between the king and the shepherd boy had started out very amicably. David was the only person who could, by playing upon his harp and singing, soothe Saul during the fits of depression to which the king was prone. As David grew to manhood, Saul eventually appointed him a commander in his army.

Saul was a great warrior, and had been chosen by God and anointed by the prophet Samuel to be the first king of Israel. However, Saul did not hold fast to his faith in the Lord and fell into idolatry. The Lord turned away from him and directed Samuel to locate David, son of Jesse of Bethlehem, and appoint him king of Israel. This Samuel did reluctantly, some time before David met Goliath, and although David was not aware that he had been anointed the future king of Israel, he did know that he was filled with the spirit of the Lord (**I Samuel 16:1-13**).

As time went by, as the tale of David's successes in battle was told again and again, the women began to sing, "Saul has killed his thousands, but David has killed his ten thousands." Saul's reaction was fear; he reasoned that, since David had the hearts of the people, they would soon make David king and depose him. Saul set about to get rid of David.

All of Saul's plots and plans to kill David failed, and, as it happened, the fact that Saul opposed him only endeared this young hero more to the people. Saul's own son, Jonathan, developed a life-long friendship with David. Saul's relentless pursuit also forced David gather men around himself for his own protection, and his little army slowly grew. After numerous attempts at reconciliation with Saul failed, David eventually formed an alliance with Israel's arch-enemy, Achish, the Philistine king of Gath.

Ashish gave David the town of Ziklag as his home; David lived there while he continued to build his army from Israelites who were opposed to Saul. This army lived by thieving upon the tribes of the Negreb, which proved to be a great mistake, as the long-suffering tribes took the first opportunity that David and his men were gone to destroy Ziklag and abduct David's family. David pursued and massacred them, recovering his two wives and children.

Soon thereafter word came to David of Saul and Jonathan's deaths in battle (**II Samuel 1:1-4**). A messenger brought Saul's crown and bracelet and laid them at David's feet. David composed a beautiful ode—a *"lamentation over Saul and over Jonathan his Son"* (**II Samuel 1:17-27**), which he decreed was to be taught to all children of Judah to honor Jonathan and Saul's memory. This was only one of many songs that David would write, more than eighty of which are gathered into the Book of Psalms, one of the books of poetry of the Old Testament.

One of the first things David did after gaining the kingship of Israel was to recover the Ark of the Covenant, which had fallen into the hands of the Philistines, and take it to Jerusalem, which he made the political and religious capital of Israel (**II Samuel 6: 1-19**). (David's triumphant entrance into Jerusalem with the Ark has been interpreted as foretelling Christ's entry into the city, prior to the Passion.) Having the Ark in Jerusalem meant that God Himself was there, consecrating it as a Holy City.

David reigned as king of Israel for forty and one-half years; his behavior was not without blemish (he stole Bathsheba from her husband Uriah, and he was indulgent to the point of weakness with his sons, especially Absalom), but he passed a great legacy on to his son Solomon. David died (in 1015 BCE) at the age of seventy years; according to tradition, he is buried on Mount Zion, in the city of Jerusalem.

Templates for King David's Crown

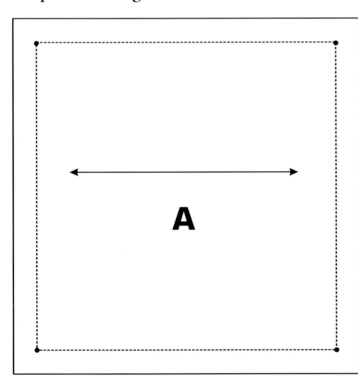

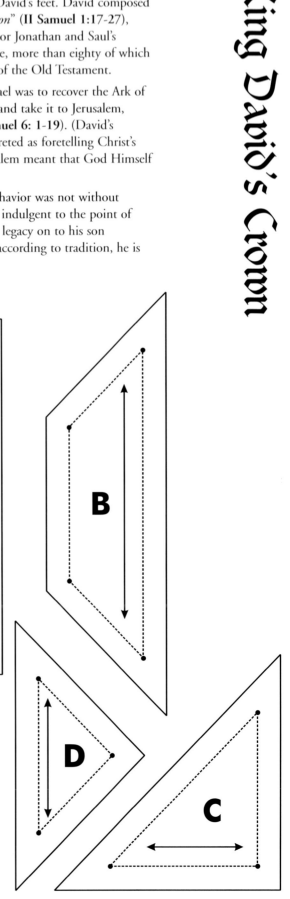

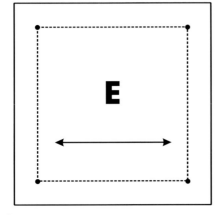

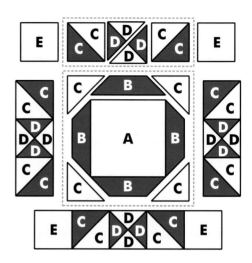

Cut the following to make one block:

Fabric	Template	Cut	Yield	Instructions
Light	A	1	-	Template A
Dark	B	4	-	Template B
Light	C	12	-	Template C
Dark	C	8	-	Template C
Light	D	8	-	Template D
Dark	D	8	-	Template D
Light	E	4	-	Template E

King David's Crown (finishes 8")

Because there is one odd shaped piece in the design that cannot be rotary-cut, it is best to use templates.

1. Using the technique described in the "Hints and Tips" section on page 67 and the templates on the next page, cut out all the pieces needed for the block.

2. Sew the dark odd shaped pieces (B) to the center square (A).

3. Align light triangles (C) with corner of center unit, sew.

4. Assemble the four "side" units:

   a. Sew the light and dark triangles (D) into pairs. Sew pairs into square units.

   b. Join the remaining light and dark triangles (C) into pairs. Sew a unit to opposite sides of the square units; make four strips

5. Attach a strip to opposite sides of the center square.

6. To the remaining two strips sew the light squares (E) to each end. Attach to top and bottom of unit to finish.

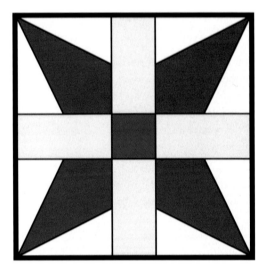

Widely recognized as one of the most remarkable books in the Bible for its magnificent language, provocative content, and stunning climax, the book of Job is one of "wisdom" writings of the Israelites, along with Proverbs and Ecclesiastes. A great diversity of opinion exists as to its authorship— from the similarity of sentiment and language to that of Psalms and Proverbs, it is supposed by some to have been written in the time of David and Solomon. Others argue that it was written by Job himself, or perhaps more probably by Moses, who was "*learned in all the wisdom of the Egyptians, and mighty in words and deeds*" (**Acts 7:22**).

Job, along with Noah and Daniel, was apparently well known in the days of the prophet Ezekiel, around 600 BCE (**Ezekiel 14:14**), and it is thought that the book was written about that time. The book of Job formed a part of the sacred Scriptures used by our Lord and His apostles, and is referred to as a part of the inspired Word (**I Corinthians 3:19**). More recently, Martin Luther spoke of it as magnificent and sublime, and Alfred Lord Tenneyson, the famous poet of the nineteenth century, called the book of Job the greatest poem of ancient and modern times.

The central subject of the book is the questioning of conventional wisdom, and it shows the blessedness of the truly pious, even amid sore afflictions, and thereby delivers comfort and hope to those believers who face terrible problems. The reader is introduced to the main character in the first verse of the first chapter of the book; Job is described as a man who has raised his family, made his place in his village and is seen as "perfect and upright."

The dramatic action of the book suddenly turns to Heaven, where a meeting is being held among God and several other beings; among them is Satan, who reports that he has been spending his time wandering to and fro across the earth. God asks him if he's had occasion to notice his righteous servant Job. Satan replies that he is unimpressed with Job's piety—after all, he has everything a person could possibly want. If he had some serious trouble in his life, Satan says, Job would not remain faithful to God. God gives Satan permission to test Job.

Job suddenly loses everything: his family, his flocks, and all he possessed. "*Then Job rose, and rent his mantle, and shaved his head and fell down upon the ground, and worshiped, and said, 'Naked came I out of my Mother's womb, and naked shall I return thither: the Lord gave, and the Lord hath taken away; blessed be the name of the Lord.' In all this Job sinned not, nor charged God foolishly*" (**Job 1:20-22**).

Satan again plots against Job and gives him a terrible disease, causing him great pain. Then begins a long and tortured poetic struggle between Job and three of his good friends—Eliphaz, Zophar, and Bildad—to try and understand why Job's fortunes have changed so dramatically; the friends are convinced that Job has sinned in some way, and is possibly not aware of it. Job insists on his innocence and expresses a strong desire to meet God face-to-face so that he might determine the reason for his suffering.

The story concludes with a dramatic confrontation, when God speaks to Job out of a whirl-wind. Job at last has a firsthand experience with God; he sees him directly. No longer is his knowledge of God secondhand, and Job knows that the "conventional wisdom" that he had been hearing from his friends was not the answer for the circumstance that had been visited on him. God restores Job's material possessions to him, in even greater numbers that before his trials, and he blessed with additional children. Job is not rewarded with any new answers to the problems of suffering, but he is left with the knowledge that God is real, in spite of what seems to be unfairness in the corporal world.

This story of reward and punishment, hope and despair leaves us feeling somewhat uncomfort-able in its lesson. It exposes man's greatest fear, that the God of Love we trust might intention-ally bring misfortune to test our loyalty and faith. But thoughtful reasoning ultimately brings us to the realization that faith is a gift we must pray for, and that we cannot judge all events from our perspective of limited understanding. "*My friends scorn me but mine eyes poureth out tears unto God*" (**Job 6:20**).

Connector Rectangles - Ice Cream Cones

Here's an easy, quick method for making the four main motifs for this design.

1. Determine finished size of unit needed, cut base and Connector fabric to that mesaurement. Place right sides together with the "Connector" on top.

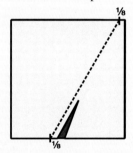

2. Place a mark 1/8" in from the upper right edge.

3. Fold unit in half to determine center line. Place a second mark 1/8" to the left of that mark on the bottom edge.

4. Draw a line connecting the two marks and sew along the line.

5. Trim the excess Connector fabric from the right side of the sewn line, leaving 1/4" seam allowance.

6. Fold the Connector fabric over the seam and press.

7. Trim the Connector fabric to edges of base fabric as illustrated by dotted line.

8. Rotate the unit counter clockwise so that the finished Connector is now on top.

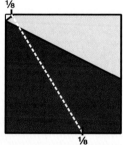

9. Repeat the process from the left edge; place the top mark 1/8" in from the left top edge and the bottom mark 1/8" to the right of the center line.

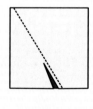
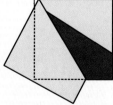

10. Stitch, trim, fold Connector fabric back over seam allowance and press.

11. Trim to complete block.

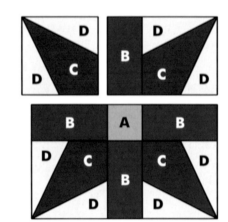

Cut the following to make one block:

Fabric	Template	Cut	Yield	Instructions
Medium	A	1	-	2" Square
Dark1	B	4	-	2 x 3¾" Rectangles
Dark2	C	4	-	3¾" Square (or Template C)
Light	D	8	-	3¾" Connector Square (or Template D)

Job's Tears (finishes 8")

1. Following the instructions on page 28, make four corner units using the dark2 (C) and light (D) fabrics squares.

2. Sew dark1 rectangles (B) to opposite sides of the medium center square (A) to make center strip.

3. Attach a corner units to opposite sides of the two remaining dark1 rectangles (B) to make top and bottom strips.

4. Join the three strips together as illustrated to complete the block.

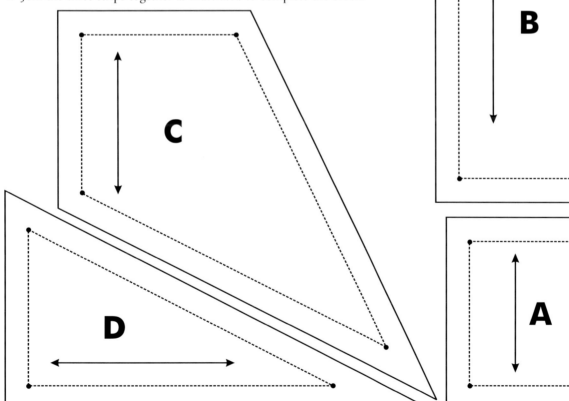

Bethlehem Star

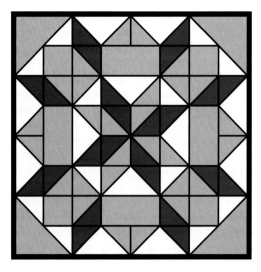

The story of the birth of Jesus and the three wise men who came seeking Him from a faraway country is one of the most cherished of the Christian faith. The three, who may have been astrologers from Persia, traveled to Jerusalem, guided by an unusually bright star. Various prophecies had foretold the coming of a new ruler for Israel, and the "wise men" (magi) believed this star was a fulfillment of the prophecies. As they inquired as to the whereabouts of the new, infant, king of the Jews, word of their search reached Herod, the then-current ruler. He, understandably, was not pleased at the discovery of a new monarch; he himself was the king of the Jews, and no new son had been born to him. Herod held an audience with the three magi, and told them to let him know when they found this new king, as he also wanted to go and worship him.

Having accomplished nothing in Jerusalem, the magi set out for Bethlehem, and saw the star halt over the building where the baby lay in a feed trough. "*When they had heard the king, they departed; and lo, the star, which they saw in the East, went before them, till it came and stood over where the young child was. When they saw the star, they rejoiced with exceeding great joy*" (**Matthew 2:9-10**). They knelt and worshiped him, and offered their gifts of gold, frankincense and myrrh. Then, rather than returning to Jerusalem, the three took another route home, having been warned in a dream not to return to Herod. Some accounts say that each of them— Balthassar, Mechior, and Gaspar—later became kings. As for Herod, he was infuriated at their betrayal and subsequently ordered that all the male infants in the area of Bethlehem be killed. (Many Bible scholars point out the similarity of the New Testament story of Herod and Jesus to the Old Testament story of Pharaoh and Moses; these scholars believe the repetition of theme to be a deliberate way of pointing out that those who followed Jesus were taking part in a new exodus—again, from slavery [of sin] to freedom [through eternal life].)

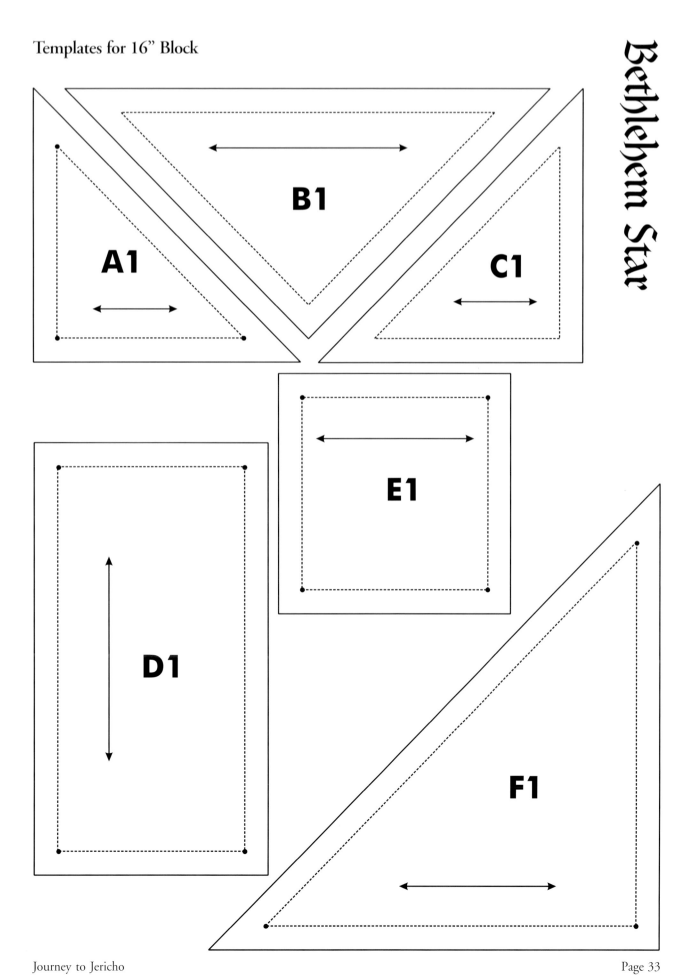

Bethlehem Star

A1

B1

C1

E1

D1

F1

Lily of the Field

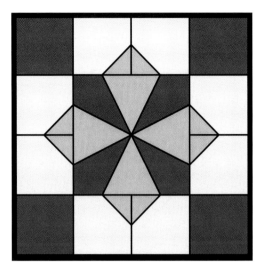

P alestine was, from all descriptions, an especially beautiful country during the time in which many of the stories of the Bible are set. Small in area (only about 150 miles long, and about half that wide), it is centered by a long mountain range that stretches from Galilee in the north to the Negeb desert in the south. To one side of the mountain range is the Mediterranean; it was on the coastal plain that much of the ancient population lived—there, and in the fertile Jezreel Valley that wound through the mountains from the ocean's edge. On the other side of the mountains is the great Rift Valley through which the Jordan River flows; headwaters of the river are in the Syrian mountains—it descends to and through the Sea of Galilee, then empties into the Dead Sea, a great land-locked saltwater ocean. The topography changes from humid and fertile around Galilee to dry and desert-like near the Dead Sea. In ancient times, the mountainsides were heavily forested with timber, and date palms were grown in the Dead Sea region and all along the Jordan River. Farmers cultivated pomegranates, wheat, barley, figs, olive trees, and grapevines.

The earth and water alike were filled with flowers, which provided great inspiration to the artisans of the Old Testament. In the description of the lavish building which Solomon erected as the Lord's Only Temple, an outer courtyard is said to have contained a basin "whose brim was made like the brim of a cup, like the flower of a lily." *There is a description of the tops of pillars (the capitals) being done in "lily-work"* (**I Kings 7:26, 22**). Architectural historians believe that the lily that inspired this decoration was the water lily, or lotus, because it has large white flowers streaked with pink—perfect for being rendered in marble.

The Hebrew word for "whiteness," shoshan, was a kind of catch-all term used to describe all sorts of flowers native to the area: crocus, tulip, iris, anemone, gladiolus, ranunculus, even a predecessor of what we know as the Easter lily. The word has been translated to appear as "lily of the valley" in **Song of Solomon 2:1-2**, **16**, **6:2-3**, and **7:2**.

This should not be taken to mean that the flowers were always white—the anemone, which grew wild over much of the area, comes in many jewel-like colors. It is probably the flower that Jesus used to illustrate one of the most beloved of all Bible verses: "*Consider the lilies how they grow: they neither toil nor spin; yet I tell you, even Solomon in all his glory was not arrayed like one of these*" (**Luke 12:27**): alternatively, from **Matthew 6:28-29**; "*And why are you anxious about clothing? Consider the lilies of the field, how they grow; they neither toil nor spin; yet I tell you, even Solomon in all his glory was not arrayed like one of these.*" As He described how completely God takes care of those who believe in Him, Jesus could well have been looking across a field of purple, blue, red, white, and wine-colored anemones. Their large, poppy-like blooms sit atop rather skimpy stems with airy, fern-like foliage. It was called "windflower" by the Greeks; in other uses, it was called "lily."

The lily is the emblem of purity, and as such, has become associated with the Virgin Mary. Occasionally, the Infant Christ is represented offering a spray of lilies to a saint, symbolizing chastity. Few would disagree that the lily is more closely associated with the sacred, and by extension with worship, than perhaps any other flower—the reason, no doubt, that early quilters chose this patchwork block to represent the "Lily of the Field."

Templates for Lily of the Field Block

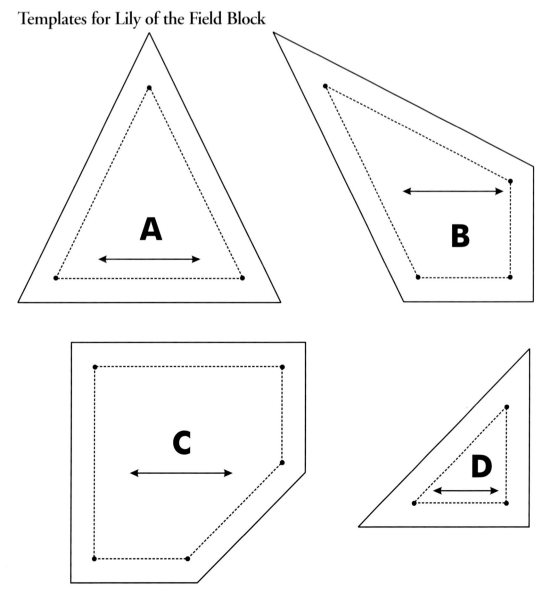

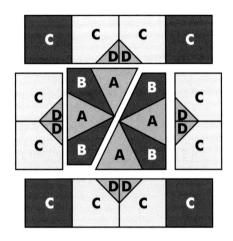

Cut the following to make one block:

Fabric	Template	Cut	Yield	Instructions
Medium	A	4		Template A
Dark	B	4		Template B
Light	C	8		2½" Squares
Dark	C	4		2½" Squares
Medium	D	8		1½" Connector Squares

Lily of the Field (finishes 8")

1. Make the center square.

   a. Following diagram above, sew a medium triangle (A) to a dark piece (B) along the long sides, making 4 AB units. Sew these units into pairs, then sew the two units together to form the center square.

2. Make side strips.

   a. Sew medium Connector squares (D) to the light base squares (C) as illustrated on page 45.

   b. Join the squares into pairs, Connector corners together.

3. Sew two of the strips to opposite sides of the center square.

5. To the remaining to strips add the dark squares (C) to each end.

6. Sew the strips to top and bottom to complete block.

Many of the best-known events of Jesus' ministry on earth took place along the shores of the Sea of Galilee. It was near the seaside town of Capernaum that Jesus delivered the Sermon on the Mount; the miracle of the loaves and fishes took place *"up in the hills, along the Sea of Galilee"* (**Matthew 15:29-39**, see also **Luke 9:10-17**). It was on the opposite shore that the healing of one (or, possibly, two) demon-possessed men took place—the evil spirits, knowing they were to be cast out, begged to be sent into a nearby herd of pigs, which then stampeded into the water and drowned themselves. (**Matthew 8:28-32**; also, **Luke 8:26-33**)

It was from the shores of the Sea of Galilee that Jesus conscripted his first four disciples: *"As he walked by the Sea of Galilee, he saw two brothers, Simon who is called Peter and Andrew his brother, casting a net into the sea, for they were fishermen. And he said to them, 'Follow me, and I will make you fishers of men.' Immediately they left their nets and followed him. And going on from there he saw two other brothers, James the son of Zebedee and John his brother, in the boat with Zebedee their father, mending their nets and he called them. Immediately they left the boat and their father and followed him. And he went about all Galilee, teaching in their synagogues and preaching the gospel of the kingdom. . ."* (**Matthew 4:18-23**).

Ancient history records fierce storms on the sea, which is actually a large lake—it measures about 12½ miles long by about seven miles wide—through which the River Jordan flows. There are two accounts of Jesus calming the weather on the lake.

"But as they sailed, he fell asleep and there came down a storm of wind on the lake; and they were filled with water, and were in jeopardy. And they came to Him and awoke Him saying, 'Master, Master, we perish.' Then he arose and rebuked the wind and the raging of the water; and they ceased, and there was a calm" (**Luke 8:23-24**).

Only the smallest details are different in the account given in **Mark 4:37-41**:*"And there arose a great storm of wind, and the waves beat into the ship, so that it was now full. And He was in the hinder part of the ship asleep on a pillow: and they awake Him, and say unto Him, 'Master, carest thou not that we perish?' And He arose, and rebuked the wind and said unto the sea, 'Peace, be still.' And the wind ceased, and there was a great calm. And He said unto them, 'Why are ye so fearful? How is it that ye have no faith?' And they feared exceedingly, and said one to another,*

Storm at Sea

'What manner of Man is this, that even the wind and the sea obey Him?"

Even though, or perhaps because, their lives centered around the sea, fishermen like Peter regarded these terrifying storms with great respect. There is the story of Peter and the other disciples trying to sail their boat across the Sea of Galilee in a headwind, when they spotted a figure that looked like Jesus walking on top of the water. Because they had not seen their Lord in four days, they weren't certain that the figure was not a ghost. To prove that the figure was actually Jesus, Peter asked that the Lord make it possible for him to walk on the water also. "*He said, 'Come.' So Peter got out of the boat and walked on the water and came to Jesus; but when he saw the wind, he was afraid, and beginning to sink, he cried out, 'Lord, save me'*" (**Matthew 14:22-32**). This passage, taken with the others, only underline the fear with which the people of Jesus' time regarded a "Storm at Sea."

Quilters have chosen a patchwork block with nothing but straight seams as their "Storm at Sea." The contrasting fabrics, and the way the angles between them change, create a sensation of wave-like movement so convincing, we keep checking the design to reassure ourselves that there are really no curves!

Templates for Storm at Sea Block

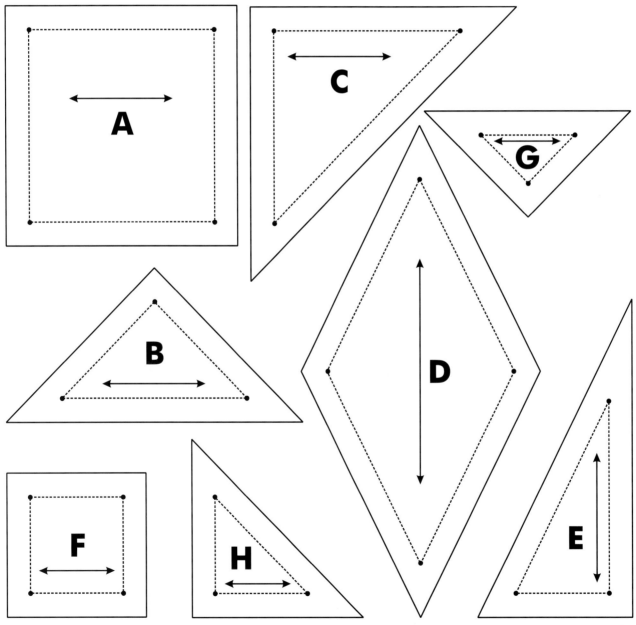

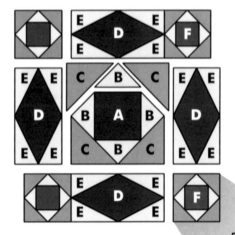

Cut the following to make one block...

Fabric	Template	Cut	Yield	Instructions
Dark1	A	1		2½" Square
Light triangles	B	1	4	3¼" Square, Cut twice diagonally into quarter-square
Medium	C	2	4	2⅞" Squares, Cut diagonally into half-square triangles
Dark1	D	4		Template D
Light	E	16		Template E (cut 8 as is, cut 8 with template reversed)
Dark2	F	4		1½" Squares
Light triangles	G	4	16	2¼" Squares, Cut twice diagonally into quarter-square
Medium	H	8	16	1⅞" Squares, Cut diagonally into half-square triangles

Storm at Sea (finishes 8")

1. Make the center square...

    a. Following diagram above, sew the light quarter-square triangles (B) to dark1 center square (A). Note: Be careful, as the outside edges will be on the bias and can easily stretch.

    b. Attach the medium half-square triangles (C) to all four sides to complete center square.

2. Sew the four light triangles (E) to the dark1 piece (D) to make a rectangle.

3. Sew two of the strips to opposite sides of the center square.

5. Make the four corner units...

    a. Following small diagram above, sew the light quarter-square triangles (G) to dark2 center square (F). (The note from 1a applies here as well.)

    b. Attach the medium half-square triangles (H) to all four sides to complete corner units.

6. Sew the corner units to both ends of the remaining two side strips.

7. Sew the strips to top and bottom to complete block.

Hosanna

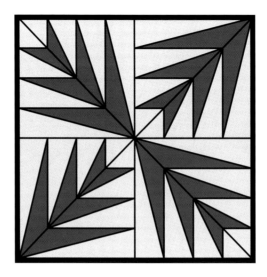

Palm Sunday is one of the great days of joy for Christians. It marks the beginning of Holy Week, the culmination of which is Easter. Palm Sunday celebrates the day that Jesus made his triumphant entry into Jerusalem, riding on a donkey, thereby fulfilling an ancient prophecy:

> *"Rejoice greatly, O daughter of Zion!*
> *Shout aloud, O daughter of Jerusalem!*
> *Lo, your king comes to you:*
> *triumphant and victorious is he,*
> *humble and riding on an ass,*
> *on a colt, the foal of an ass."*

Zechariah 9:9

As Jesus rode into Jerusalem, the crowd shouted "Hosanna" to him and sang songs from **Psalms 118:25-26**: "*Save now, I beseech thee, O Lord: O Lord, I beseech thee, send now prosperity. Blessed be he that cometh in the name of the Lord: we have blessed you out of the house of the Lord.*" (Although we have come to think of "hosanna" as a praise word, its original meaning was "save us.") As the crowd called to Jesus, many of them believed he had come as a new ruler of Palestine, whose term would begin immediately, thereby delivering them from the harsh rule of the Roman government.

Other prophecies had predicted that the "son of David," the "King of Israel" would reclaim Jerusalem for God; therefore, the faithful laid their cloaks and branches of the palm tree along the road, as would befit a king: "*a great crowd who had come to the feast [of the Passover] heard that Jesus was coming to Jerusalem. So they took branches of palm trees and went out to meet him, crying, 'Hosanna! Blessed is he who comes in the name of the Lord, even the King of Israel!*'" (**John 12:12-13**). And from Matthew comes this account: "*. . . they brought the ass and the colt, and put their garments on them, and he sat thereon. Most of the crowd spread their garments on the road, and others cut branches from the trees and spread them on the road. And the crowds that went before him and that followed him shouted, 'Hosanna to the Son of David! Blessed is he who comes in the name of the Lord! Hosanna in the highest!' And when he entered Jerusalem, all the city was stirred, saying, 'Who is this?' And the crowds said, 'This is the prophet Jesus from Nazareth of Galilee'*" (**Matthew 21:7-11**).

The "branches from the trees" were very likely from the date palm, which is emblematic of Palestine. Palm trees are described as "*flourishing*" (**Psalms 92:12**), and "*upright*" (**Jeremiah 10:5**). In the olden days, Jericho was named "*the city of palm trees*" (**Deuteronomy 34:3**). The trees can grow to as much as 100 feet tall, with an average height of 40 or 50 feet; that great height allows the growth of very long fronds (best described as a leaf the size of a branch), six to twelve feet long. It is usually ten years before a date palm begins to bear fruit, but then each year it produces six to ten clusters of fruit, each containing hundreds of dates. The fruit is harvested by climbers who scale the trunk of the tree, carrying large knives to sever the stems of the clusters of dates; once dried, dates do not spoil, and they were a lightweight, nourishing diet staple on the camel caravans that criss-crossed the desert. To those who know how to accomplish it, climbing a palm tree is not a challenge; it is easy to imagine a number of eager youths skinnying up palm trees to cut the opulent fronds for the excited crowds lining the road into Jerusalem.

The tree is the symbol of the righteous (**Psalms 92:12**). At the institution of the Feast of Tabernacles (**Leviticus 23:40**), palm leaves were proscribed as part of the foliage to be carried by those appearing joyfully before the presence of the Lord, and apparently it was a very important part, since the Hebrew word, lulabh, meaning palm, was the liturgical name given that bunch of green branches.

Palm branches were symbolic of victory (**Revelation 7:9**), and it is the "*victory*" meaning that was carried into Christian symbolism, where the palm branch was used to suggest the martyr's triumph over death. Martyrs are often depicted with the palm either in place of, or in addition to, the instruments of their martyrdom. Christ is often shown bearing the palm branch as a symbol of His triumph over sin and death.

A palm tree staff is the attribute of St. Christopher, in reference to the legend that he uprooted a palm tree to support himself on his travels. After carrying Christ across the river, he thrust the staff into the ground, whereupon it took root and bore fruit. A dress made of palm leaves is an attribute of St. Paul the hermit.

In many Christian denominations, the palm branches used in Palm Sunday services are ritually burned and the ashes are saved to be used for the following year's Ash Wednesday services. Ash Wednesday is the first day of Lent; tradition calls the faithful to church for the imposition of ashes on the forehead, a ritual signifying the penitence of the supplicant. The ashes represent the death of the human body and symbolize the shortness of earthly life; Lent is a time during which the faithful either practice symbolic acts of self-denial or study in order to draw closer to Christ in this time leading up to Holy Week.

The quilt pattern of palm leaves known as "Hosanna" was pre-Revolutionary in origin. It is possible that an early American woman was inspired by a hymn written specifically for Palm Sunday in 1823 by Henry Hart Milman:

> "*Ride on! Ride on in Majesty!*
> *Hark! all the tribes hosanna cry:*
> *Thy humble beast pursues his road*
> *with palms scatter'd, garments strowed.*
> *Ride on! Ride on in majesty!*
> *In lowly pomp ride on to die;*
> *O Christ, Thy triumph begin*
> *o'er captive death and conquer'd sin.*"

Few patterns can rival "Hosanna" for its graphic and realistic representation, and it is a most fitting way to signify that Christ is in one's heart and home.

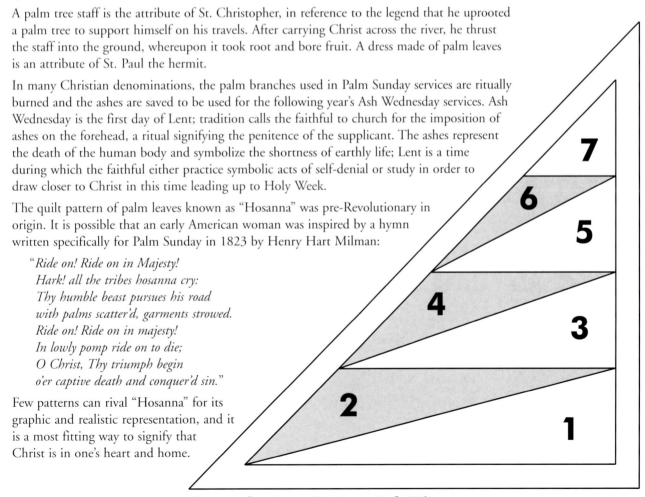

Pattern for Paper Piecing - Left Side

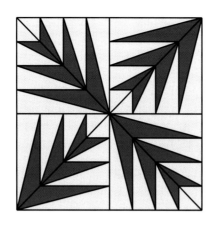

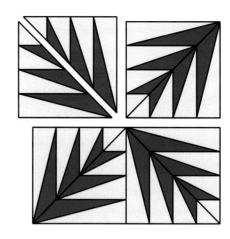

Cut the following to make one block...

Fabric	Piece	Cut	Yield	Instructions
Light				1½" Strips
Dark				1½" Strips

Hosanna (finishes 8")

Paper piecing makes piecing this block extremely accurate.

1. Copy the left and right sides of the patterns for paper piecing onto a suitable foundation material (newsprint, paper foundation material, etc.). Make a copy for each "frond" you will make. Each paper pattern is used only one time.

2. Lay a strip of light fabric right side up across the section labeled "1". Ensure that is covers the entire area and extends at least ¼" beyond the lines bounding the area. Line the top of the strip ¼" over the line dividing section 1 and 2 (Diagram 1).

3. Lay a strip of the dark fabric right side down over the light strip; align the top edges. Pin through all layers avoiding the stitching line (Diagram 2).

4. Turn the unit over to back and stitch on the line dividing the two sections.

5. Turn right side up and trim seam allowance to ¼". Press the dark fabric open (Diagram 3).

6. Continue adding strips as in steps 2 through 5, alternating light and dark (Diagram 4).

7. Trim unit, leaving ¼" seam allowance all around (outer line).

8. Join a left and right section together to make sub-blocks.

9. Sew the four sub-blocks together to finish your block.

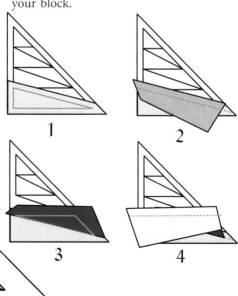

Pattern for Paper Piecing - Right Side

Other than the Cross itself, no other image of Christ's Passion is more poignant than the Crown of Thorns. "*And the soldiers clothed him with purple and plaited a crown of thorns and put it about His head and began to salute him, 'Hail, King of the Jews.'*" (**Mark 15:17-18**).

Jesus, accused of heresy by the politically motivated temple priests of Jerusalem, was brought to trial before the Roman emperor, Pontius Pilate. Upon direct questioning from Pilate, "*Are you the King of the Jews?*", He answered, "*You have said so*" (**Mark 25:20**), and offered nothing else in His own defense. He knew that He and Pilate were speaking different languages—not literally, but figuratively.

Scholars point out that the word "king" is significant in this usage. Jesus had been asked earlier, when he was brought up before the corrupt priests, if he was "Christ, the Son of the Blessed," and he had answered "*I am*" (**Mark 14:62**). The word "king," chosen deliberately by Pilate, indicated a ruler who dictated to and enslaved their subjects. Jesus refused to be caught in Pilate's verbal trap.

Pilate himself would later be recalled to Rome because of his own abuse of power (he had a number of Samaritans killed as they were on their annual pilgrimage to Jerusalem for one of the High Holy Days). He was a brutal ruler and had already been involved in several disputes with the Jews; he was determined to quell any signs of unrest in order that his own career would not be adversely affected.

The fact that Jerusalem was under Roman military occupation made the city a tinderbox; the Jews were afraid that if any one incident brought too much attention onto them, the Romans would come and destroy them, "*both our holy place and our nation. But one of them, Caiaphas, who was a high priest that year, said to them, 'You know nothing at all; you do not understand that it is expedient for you that one man should die for the people, and that the whole nation should not perish*" (**John 11:46-50**). Said another way, Caiaphas was urging them to get rid of the troublemaker Jesus, rather than risking another run-in with the Roman military. Thus the maneuvering of the temple priests led to civil charges against Jesus, and Pilate was put in position to pass judgment.

Crown of Thorns

Despite Pilate's appearing to try to take the middle road at Jesus' trial, we must resist the inclination to think better of him than he deserves. Some accounts make Pilate seem sympathetic toward Jesus and confused by the malice directed toward Him; we could be swayed by the fact that Pilate offered the crowd the opportunity to set Jesus free (they chose to liberate the murderer Barabbas instead). As we read the story of the Passion, we must keep in mind that Pilate represents the forces of evil - in the end, it was he who wrote out the *titulus*, or notice, that was hung around Jesus' neck as he carried his cross. The titulus, in Pilate's own hand, was written in Hebrew, Latin, and Greek: after hanging about His neck, it was nailed above His head on the cross, "Jesus the Nazarene, King of the Jews."

Pontius Pilate is the one who gave the order that Jesus be turned over to the military for crucifixion. Playing in part to the crowd, perhaps, the soldiers began to ridicule Jesus, dressing him in the purple of royalty, and crowning him with a circlet made of excruciatingly painful, piercing thorns. Degrading acts of barbarous, petty cruelty were customary in the Roman treatment of prisoners, and Jesus undoubtedly knew that this gratuitous torture would be part of his treatment. It is generally believed that Christ was compelled to wear the crown of thorns as he struggled to carry the cross to Golgotha, and it was on His head until He died. It was not lifted from His brow until He was taken down from the Cross and prepared for burial.

Some botanists believe that the crown of thorns was made of branches of the *Zizyphus spina Christi*, or jujube, tree. Another name for the tree, which overruns a great part of the Jordan Valley, is the lotus tree (which is a bit of a mystery, because it bears no resemblance to the water lily known at the lotus). The jujube tree produces thorns that are long, sharp, curved, and coated with a substance that often causes a wound to fester—it is a thoroughly nasty botanical specimen.

"By the cross, the nail, the thorn, piercing spear, and torturing scorn, Christ redeemed us. Our debt before God is canceled, for God set it aside, 'nailing it to the cross" (**Colossians 2:14**). Few of our patchwork patterns are as unmistakably representative of their name as "Crown of Thorns." The spiked wreath of triangles is not abstract—we immediately understand the design's meaning.

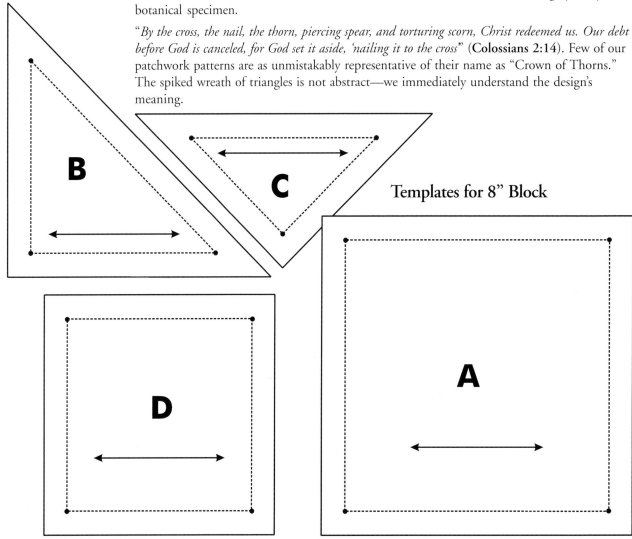

Templates for 8" Block

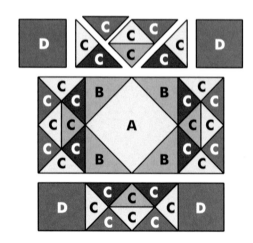

Cut the following to make one block:

Fabric	Template	Cut	Yield	8"	16"	Instructions
Light	A	1		4½"	8½"	Square
Medium	B	2	4	2½"	4½"	Connector Squares
Light	C	3	12	3¼"	5¼"	Squares, Cut twice diagonally into quarter-square tri's
Medium	C	1	4	3¼"	5¼"	Squares, Cut twice diagonally into quarter-square tri's
Dark	C	2	8	3¼"	5¼"	Squares, Cut twice diagonally into quarter-square tri's
Medium2	C	2	8	3¼"	5¼"	Squares, Cut twice diagonally into quarter-square tri's
Medium2	D	4		2½"	4½"	Squares

Crown of Thorns (finishes 8" or 16")

1. Sew the medium connector corners (B) to the center square (A) or use templates.

2. Assemble the "thorn" sections:

   a. Combine the light and medium quarter-square triangles (C) into pairs along the long edge of the triangle, make four.

   b. Sew two of the medium2 quarter-square triangles (C) to adjacent sides of the light triangle to form a larger triangle.

   c. Join the light and dark quarter-square triangles (C) into pairs along the shorter edges of the triangle (see illustration), make eight.

   d. Sew the triangles above to the larger triangle on the adjacent shorter sides. to make a rectangle.

3. Sew two of the rectangles to opposite sides of the center square.

4. To the two remaining units, attach a medium2 square (D) to each end.

5. Sew the strips to the top and bottom of your block to complete.

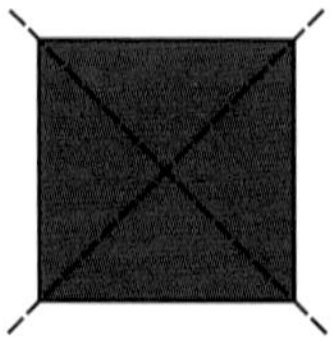

Connector Corners

Sew those corner triangles on fast...

1. Determine finished size of triangle needed.

2. Add ½".

3. Cut the square(s) to this measurement.

4. Lay the connector square onto the base fabric right sides together.

5. Mark a diagonal line through square as illustrated.

6. Sew along the line.

7. Press the fabric onto itself to form the corner triangle.

8. Trim the excess fabric leaving 1/4" seam allowance (do not cut the base fabric).

9. Repeat on other corners if needed.

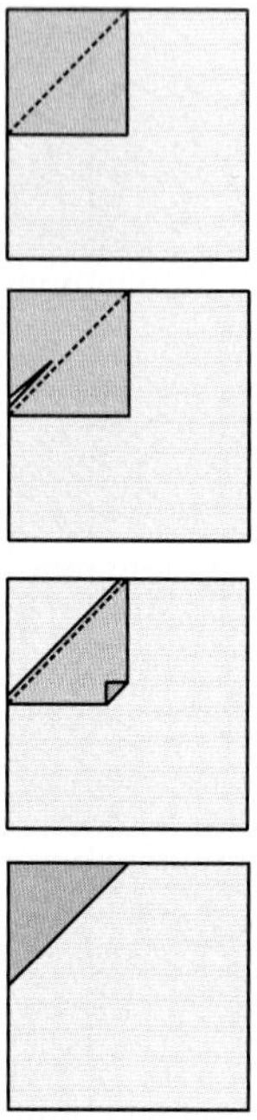

Crown of Thorns

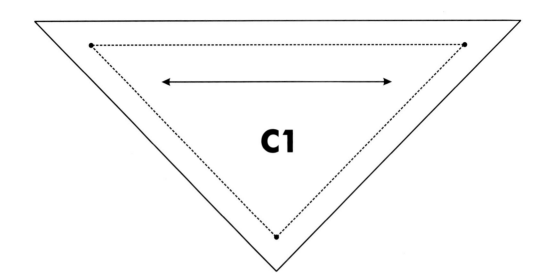

C1

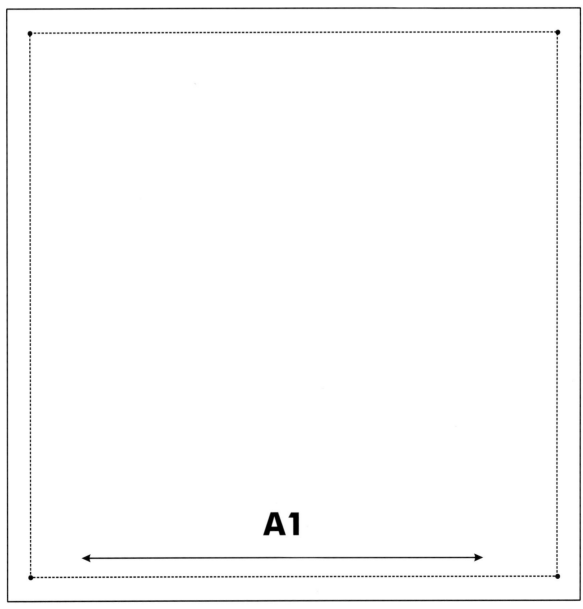

A1

Crown of Thorns

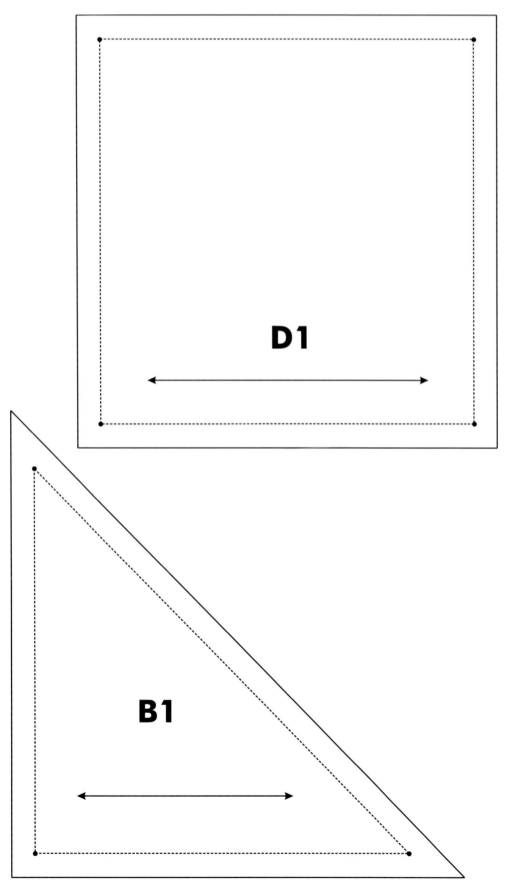

D1

B1

World Without End

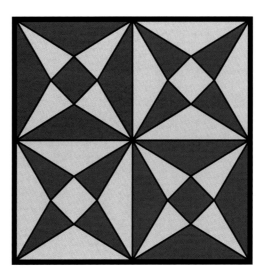

Interlinking stars are an eloquent and beautiful symbol of eternity, the true "World Without End." David, in one of his hymns, called the stars the *"handiwork of God's fingers"* (**Psalms 8:3**). And because we think of that "World Without End" as taking place above us, in heaven, it is easy to think of the network of stars as the bottom of heaven—and that one day we will fly up through the stars to unimaginable glories.

In Christian theology, the concept of eternity has two different meanings: one defines a state of being or existence that is not subject to time; the other describes an attribute of God alone. In the first meaning, eternity is timelessness, or a condition of endless duration. The other has to do with God's relation to the concept of time; some thinkers, most notably Augustine, have argued that time came into being with creation. Therefore, God created time, and, since time is a function of change, God's consciousness embraces past, present, and future in one sweeping understanding—eternity.

However vast or limited our knowledge of the concept of eternity, it is something that people of faith look forward to sharing with God at the end of their time on earth. As Augustine wrote in his Sermon 346: *"Human beings are mere scraps of life, here for only an instant... Communion with God is life, and separation from God is death. A life without eternity is unworthy of the name of life. Only eternal life is true."*

He says further, *"Immortality is a sign that man's earthly life does not exhaust its meaning; God will complete and fulfill this existence 'beyond history.' Immortality is not an inherent right or property of man, but a divine act of recreation."* Our souls are the part of our being, the spiritual entities, that survive physical death and go on to that world without end.

The phrase is found in **Isaiah 45:17**: *"But Israel shall be saved in the Lord with an everlasting salvation; ye shall not be ashamed nor confounded world without end."* It is used in the **Doxology**, which is sung in many demonominations, as well as in the liturgy of morning prayer used in Episcopal churches: *"Glory be to the Father, and to the Son, and to the Holy Ghost; as it was in the beginning, is now and ever shall be, world without end. Amen."*

Numerous and varied were the belief systems of colonial women, and church or religion was the main focus of many of their lives. That they would name a quilt block with an endlessly repetitive motif to reflect a faith in the possibility of eternal life—a "World Without End"—should come as no surprise to us two centuries later.

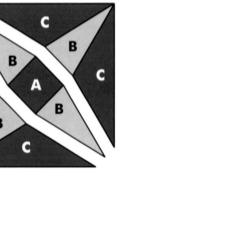

Cut the following to make one block:

Fabric	Piece	Cut	Yield	Instructions
Light	A	2		Template A
Dark	A	2		Template A
Light	B	8		Template B
Dark	B	8		Template B
Light	C	8		Template C
Dark	C	8		Template C

World Without End (finishes 8")

1. Following diagram above, attach light triangles (B) to opposite sides of the center dark square (A).

2. Sew dark triangles (C) to adjacent sides of the other two light triangles (B). Make two per block.

3. Pinning at seams, join the three units together into a square. See page 69 for information on "setting in."

4. Make two units as described and two units with colors reversed (light center square (A), dark triangles (B) and light triangles (C)).

5. Join four sub-blocks as illustrated above into your finished block.

Templates for World Without End Block

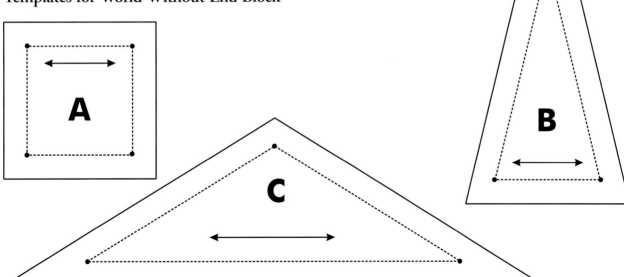

Beyond the Blocks: Making the Quilt

Setting Options

This is the layout for the original "Journey to Jericho" quilt. Smaller quilts can be made with fewer blocks, and, of course, the patterned blocks may be placed in any order you desire - they do not have to follow this arrangement. Notice that each block has been finished with a narrow border (½") of background fabric before it was set into the quilt. See the finished quilt on page 74.

The original concept for the "Journey to Jericho" quilt was that of a sampler quilt that incorporated all twelve of the Bible blocks. The patterned blocks were set diagonally with alternating unpatterned blocks, into which a plant from the Bible was quilted (see pages 54 - 60 for quilting designs).

There are many other ways, of course, to plan a quilt around any or all of these blocks. You may choose to use fewer blocks, or repeat a single block for an all-over design, or make a central medallion quilt with one of the sixteen-inch blocks (see "Joseph's Coat," "Bethlehem Star," and "Tree of Life").

Following are diagrams of some of the setting options chosen by quilters featured in the "Quilts and Their Stories" section (pages 74 - 94). Adopt one of them as your own, or study them for inspiration in planning your own layout.

A five-block quilt also benefits from a diagonal set. See the finished quilt on page 78.

A simple nine-block diagonal layout is a natural option for a square quilt. Here a variety of blocks are used; each has been bordered with a narrow strip of contrasting fabric before being set into the quilt top. See the finished quilt on page 90.

Here is a completely different approach to the five-block set. One block is repeated four times, and a different block is set into the center. Although it looks like a horizontal set when the quilt is finished, the setting diagram reveals that only a diagonal set could make the design work out. "Ohio Stars" have been incorporated as secondary motifs. See the finished quilt on page 93.

In this nine-block layout, no borders have been used around the blocks, and the repetition of a single block, each of which incorporates black, makes a simple, yet bold, statement. See the finished quilt on page 79.

The 16-inch blocks can be used singly to make a small, meaningful wallhanging. Here, a two-colored "Bethlehem Star" is set on point to make a dramatic statement in a neutral background. A very effective detail is the red border around the central block. See the finished quilt on page 78.

Another five-block set features four patchwork blocks that are exactly the same, but the center block uses the "Rose of Sharon" appliqué. Supporting blocks are each embellished with an appliquéd butterfly. (See pages 61 - 66 for appliqué patterns.) See the finished quilt on page 77.

You can combine the 16-inch blocks and the 8-inch blocks in many ways. Here is an example of the 16-inch "Tree of Life" block set on point in a central medallion configuration. Eight-inch blocks are used in the corners of the borders. See the finished quilt on page 94.

Setting Options

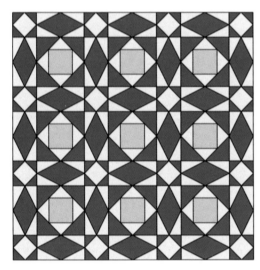

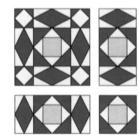

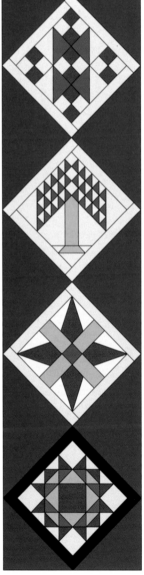

Some blocks, such as "Storm at Sea," lend themselves to "tiling" compositions—resulting an effect very much like Byzantine tile floors. When blocks are placed side by side, other patterns are produced—not just in the overall appearance. Secondary motifs sometimes pop out—in this example, four large white eight-pointed stars emerge from the nine "Storm at Sea" blocks that are set side by side. (Notice that one side section is shared by two centers—each "Storm at Sea" block must be minus one side section if the pattern is to repeat properly.) See the finished quilt on page 88.

Another possibility for setting is the six-block option, made with your choice of designs. Again, these blocks are bordered, then set on the diagonal; two plain blocks, six half-blocks, and four quarter-blocks make background. See the finished quilt on page 93.

A vertical wall-hanging, hard to beat for impact, can be made with a four-block column of blocks. You can set the blocks on the diagonal, as shown in this layout, or you can use a straight set. You will quickly realize that a diagonal set makes a longer wall hanging than the straight set—unless you add length to the straight set with borders or additional blocks. See the finished quilt on page 92.

Quilting Designs

No matter which setting option you choose for your quilt, you will have open areas in the background that can be embellished. One of the most subtle ways of adding interest to those areas is through the choice of a quilting design that is rich with meaning of its own. Presented on the following pages are six designs, all based on plants named in the Bible, for you to trace and use as quilting designs. They will fit nicely in an 8-inch block. (You could also adapt these designs to appliqué work, just as you could adapt the appliqué designs on pages 61 - 66 to quilting designs.)

The plants of the Bible are a fascinating study—more than 100 species are mentioned by name in its pages. Ancient cultures had a far more direct relationship with plants than we do today. "*I will be as the dew unto Israel; he shall grow as the lily, he shall strike root as the poplar; his shoots shall spread out; his beauty shall be like the olive, and his fragrance like Lebanon*" (**Hosea 14:5-6**). Especially during the Exodus, the children of Israel were forced to live directly off the land as they wandered "through the wilderness" from Egypt to Canaan (**Exodus 13:18**). Plants would have been a vital source of food, medicine, and fuel during those nomadic years.

In more settled times, when agriculture was possible, crops of wheat, barley, beans, and lentils were grown. Grapevines were planted so that the harvest could be eaten fresh, dried into raisins, or pressed for wine. Flax was grown for the fibrous stems, from which linen was woven, and papyrus was cultivated to make paper; it has been suggested that the Bible was written originally on papyrus.

Olives, pomegranates, and figs are mentioned many times in the Bible. "*But they shall sit every man under his vine and under his fig tree; and none shall make them afraid: for the mouth of the Lord of hosts hath spoken it*" (**Micah 4:4**). The "Tree of Knowledge" in the Garden of Eden is generally assumed to have been an apple tree, although no one knows for sure.

The cedar of Lebanon, still the national symbol of that country though few of the trees remain, is spoken of over 70 times in the Bible. Integral to Solomon's temple, it was highly prized as a building material for all important structures. After being harvested in Lebanon, the trees were floated in the Mediterranean Ocean down the Palestinian coast, then hauled overland to Jerusalem.

Herbs played an important part in daily cuisine and medical practices. Mention is made of "hyssop," which was probably very much like our marjoram, being used in the original Passover (**Exodus 12:22**); it was the twig on which the vinegar-soaked sponge was passed to Christ as he hung on the cross (**John 19:29**).

Inevitably, legends would grow up around the plants that were such a part of the daily life of early Christians, and certain ones would come to symbolize certain people, things, or attributes. Full-size drawings of six of the most beloved and most frequently mentioned plants of the Bible are presented here for you to incorporate into your quilt as you wish, thereby deepening its intrinsic meaning and adding to its beauty.

Iris

Тhe name "iris" means "sword lily," a name thought to be derived from the sorrow of Mary Magdalene at the crucifixion of Christ; as a result, it has come to be known as the flower of the Virgin, sharing the title with the lily. The iris appears as a religious symbol in the works of early Flemish masters, in which it sometimes accompanies, and sometimes replaces, the lily in pictures with the Virgin.

Fig

The fig, rather than the apple, tree is thought by some to have been the Tree of Knowledge in the Garden of Eden. It is a candidate perhaps because it appears in the story of the fall of mankind in **Genesis 3:7**, "*And the eyes of them both were opened, and they knew that they were naked; and they sewed fig leaves together and made themselves aprons.*" Subsequently, the fig became a symbol of lust, and because of the many seeds in each fruit, it also represented fertility. The fig tree bears for most of the year, far longer than most other fruit trees. "*and the stars of the sky fell to the earth as the fig tree sheds it winter fruit when shaken by a gale. . .*" (**The Revelation to St. John 6:13**).

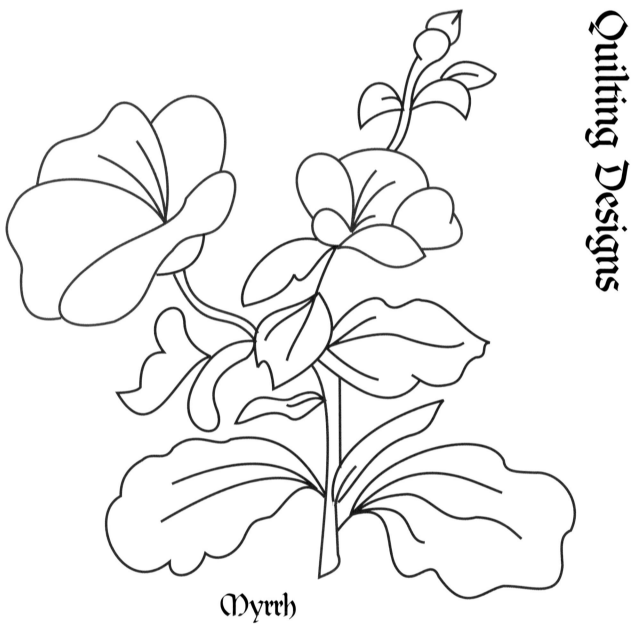

Myrrh

Many people are surprised to learn that myrrh comes from a plant. The substance brought to the infant Jesus by the Wise Men is the sap of the tree that bears its name (**Matthew 2:11**).

The first book of the Bible mentions it: "*And they[Joseph's brothers] sat down to eat bread; and they lifted up their eyes and looked, and behold, a company of Ishmaelites came from Gilead with their camels bearing spicery and balm and myrrh, going to carry it down to Egypt*" (**Genesis 37:25**). It was a component in the recipe for holy anointing oil, along with cinnamon, "aromatic cane," cassia, and olive oil given to Moses directly by God (**Exodus 30:23**). The delicate scent for which it is prized is mentioned in **Song of Solomon 5:5**—"*my fingers dripped with sweet smelling myrrh.*" In **Psalms 45:8**, it was used as a perfume for scenting clothes, in **Proverbs 7:17** to sweeten a bed, as a beauty preparation in **Esther 2:12**, and worn as body scent in **Song of Solomon 1:13**.

Myrrh was mixed with the wine at the Cross, in the customary offering given by Jews to those condemned to death; it was refused by Jesus (**Mark 15:23**). In **John 19:39**, Nicodemus presented a mixture of myrrh and aloes for Jesus' burial—"*about a hundred pounds' weight.*"

Quilting Designs

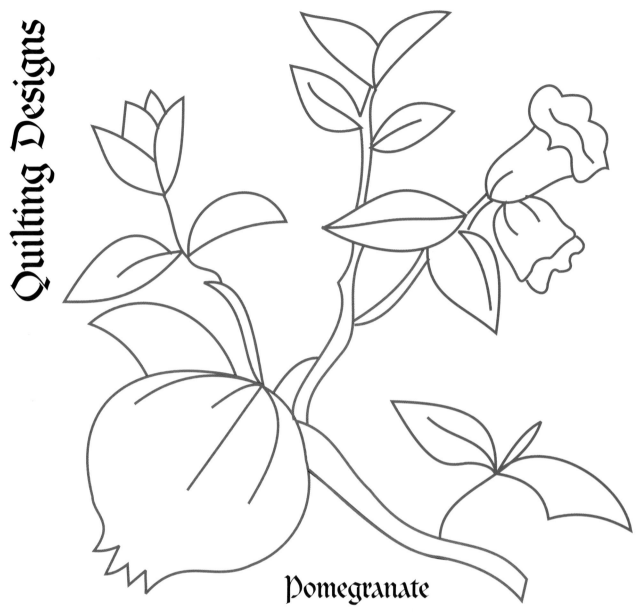

Pomegranate

The pomegranate is a fruit about the size of an orange, full of kernels contained in a tasty red pulp that may be used in a number of flavorful dishes, or crushed to yield a delicious sweet juice. The root words of its name mean "an apple full of seed." As it ripens, it peel will sometimes burst open in places from the bountiful production of seed kernels. Whenever the Bible names principal fruits or trees, the pomegranate is among them. "*For the Lord your God is bringing you into a good land, a land of brooks of water; of fountains and springs, flowing forth in valleys and hills, a land of wheat and barley, of vines and fig trees and pomegranates, a land of olive trees and honey*" (**Deuteronomy 8:7-8**). (See also **Numbers 20:5, Joel 1:12,** and **Haggai 2:19**).

A pomegranate tree at Migron is identified as the location for Saul and his army of 600 men in an Old Testament story (**I Samuel 14:20**). It was not for the possible shade it might provide, but because the pomegranate was considered sacred, that Saul chose it as a campsite before a battle with the Philistines. King Solomon chose the pomegranate to be carved 200 times into the capitals of two of the main pillars of the temple he built to the Lord in Jerusalem (**I Kings 7:20**).

There are several different meanings imparted by the pomegranate in Christian symbolism. It can stand for the power of God's Word and the riches of His grace. The bursting pomegranate symbolizes that, as Christ burst forth from the grave on Easter morning, so too will the faithful burst the bonds of death. However, the pomegranate most often represents the church, because of the unity of countless seeds in one and the same fruit.

Frankincense

The resin of a tree, as is myrrh, frankincense emits a fragrance when burned. It is one of the main ingredients in the recipe for incense the Lord dictated to Moses: "*Take sweet spices, stacte, and onycha, and galbanum, sweet spices with pure frankincense (of each shall there be an equal part), and make an incense blended as by the perfumer, seasoned with salt, pure and holy*" (**Exodus 30:34-35**). Although large quantities were imported from Sheba (**Jeremiah 6:20**), the tree is indigenous to Palestine, and some are said to still grow there.

A major difference between the aromatics frankincense and myrrh is that frankincense, apparently, can be eaten; no mention is made of eating myrrh. Frankincense was to be mixed with olive oil and used as a condiment or dressing for the grain products (bread and cereal) given as tithe to the temple; after a portion had been burned as an offering to the Lord, the remainder would be eaten by the temple priests (**Leviticus 2:1-4, 16, 6:15-16**, and **24:7**).

Because frankincense was a main ingredient of the incense used in the Temple, it has become an emblem of prayer.

Almond

The almond is a symbol of divine approval or favor; the meaning comes from the story of how the legitimate priest of the Children of Israel was chosen. God instructed to Moses to gather up a rod, or staff, from each of the twelve families of Israel and leave them overnight in the "tent of testimony." The rod of God's chosen, He promised, would sprout during the night. Next morning, Moses went into the tent, "*and, behold, the rod of Aaron for the house of Levi had sprouted and put forth buds, and produced blossoms, and it bore ripe almonds*" (**Numbers 17:1-8**). Thus it was that Aaron became the founding father of the priesthood—his sons served in the temple, and theirs after them.

The notion that almonds are a sign of divine favor has been the reason they also became a symbol of the Virgin Mary.

Yet another meaning for the almond is thought to appear in **Jeremiah 1:1-12**: "*And the word of the Lord came to me saying, 'Jeremiah, what do you see?' And I said, 'I see a rod of an almond.' Then the Lord said to me, 'You have seen well, for I am watching over my word to perform it.*" This has been interpreted to mean that, because the almond tree never sleeps—it blooms even in the winter—it is a fitting symbol of vision.

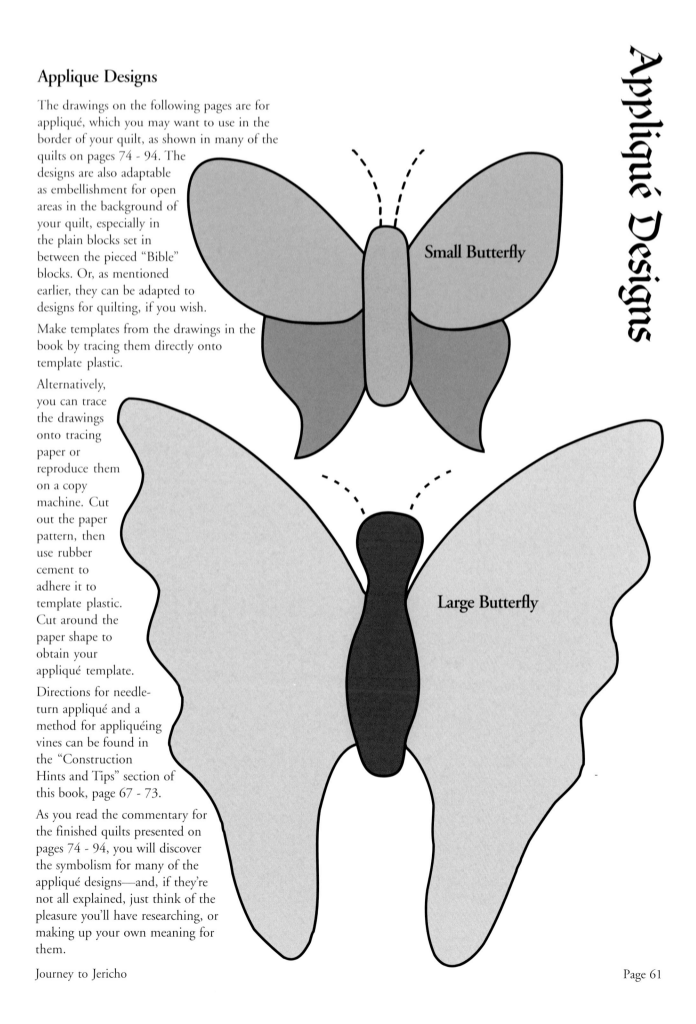

Applique Designs

The drawings on the following pages are for appliqué, which you may want to use in the border of your quilt, as shown in many of the quilts on pages 74 - 94. The designs are also adaptable as embellishment for open areas in the background of your quilt, especially in the plain blocks set in between the pieced "Bible" blocks. Or, as mentioned earlier, they can be adapted to designs for quilting, if you wish.

Make templates from the drawings in the book by tracing them directly onto template plastic.

Alternatively, you can trace the drawings onto tracing paper or reproduce them on a copy machine. Cut out the paper pattern, then use rubber cement to adhere it to template plastic. Cut around the paper shape to obtain your appliqué template.

Directions for needle-turn appliqué and a method for appliquéing vines can be found in the "Construction Hints and Tips" section of this book, page 67 - 73.

As you read the commentary for the finished quilts presented on pages 74 - 94, you will discover the symbolism for many of the appliqué designs—and, if they're not all explained, just think of the pleasure you'll have researching, or making up your own meaning for them.

Small Butterfly

Large Butterfly

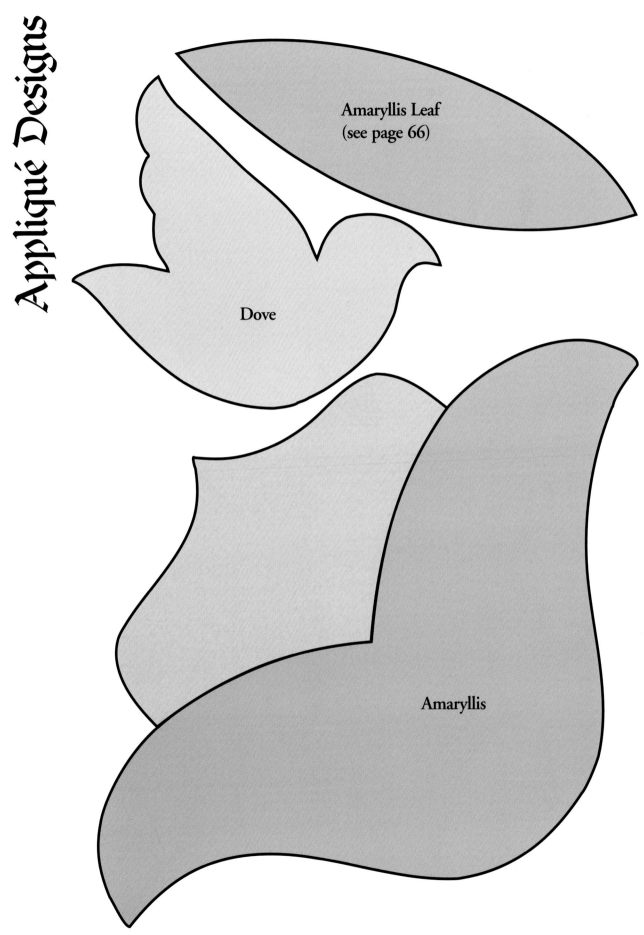

Appliqué Designs

Amaryllis Leaf
(see page 66)

Dove

Amaryllis

Indiana Rose

Indiana Rose
Leaf

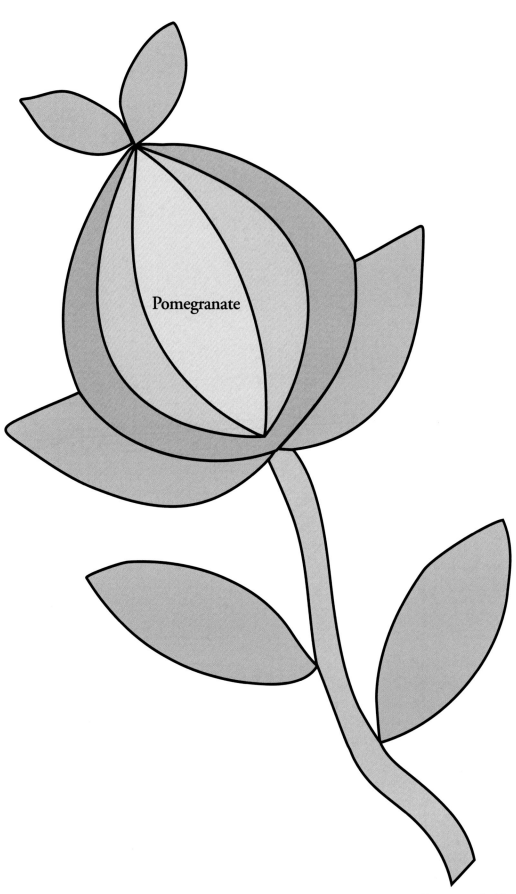

Pomegranate

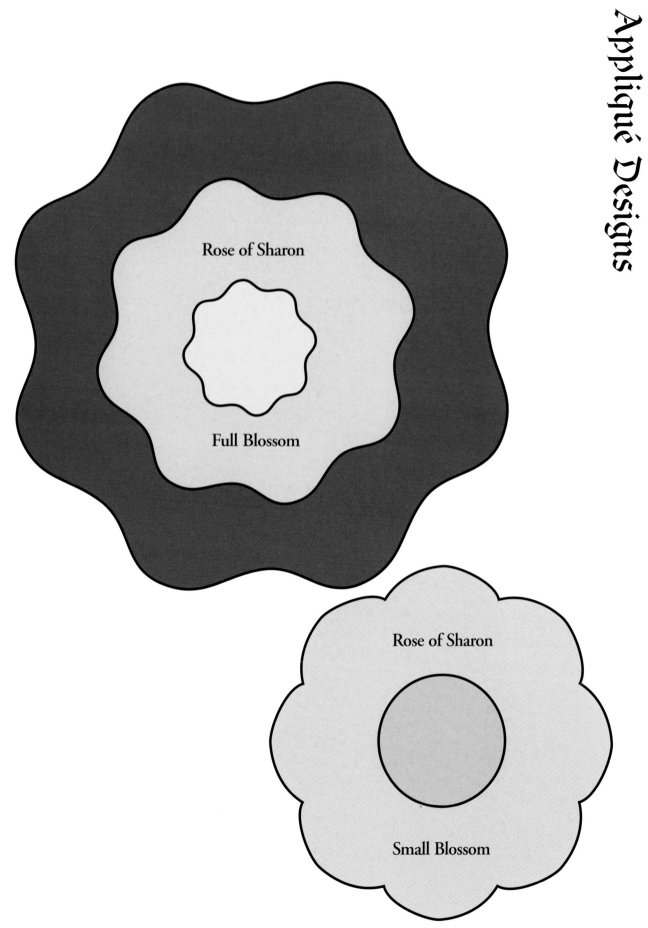

Rose of Sharon

Full Blossom

Rose of Sharon

Small Blossom

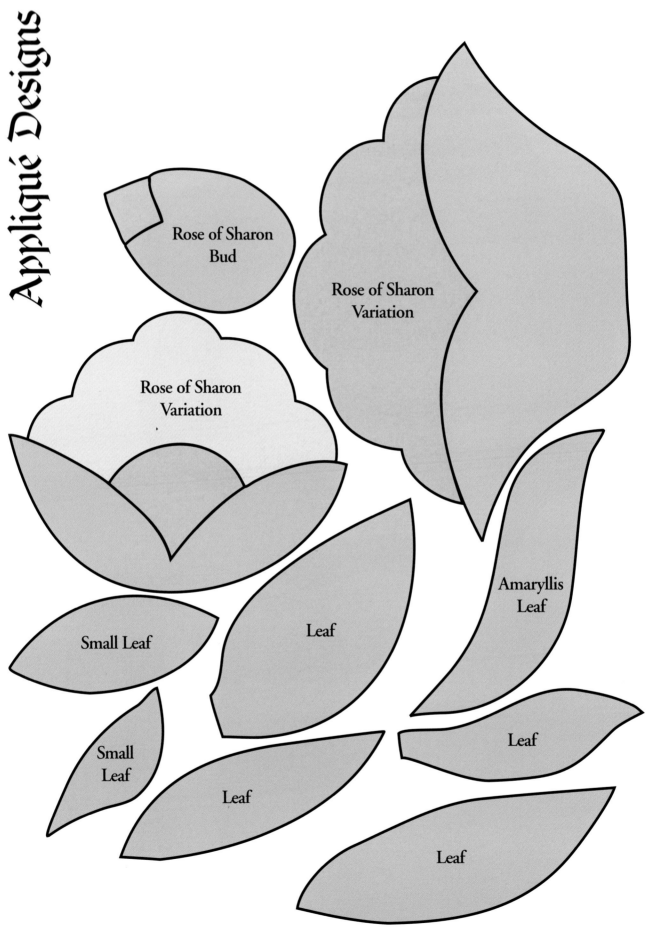

Appliqué Designs

Rose of Sharon
Bud

Rose of Sharon
Variation

Rose of Sharon
Variation

Amaryllis
Leaf

Small Leaf

Leaf

Small
Leaf

Leaf

Leaf

Leaf

Leaf

Construction Hints & Tips

Fabric Selection

Choosing fabrics for the sampler quilt that uses all twelve of the pieced blocks goes much more easily if you choose your main fabric first. If you choose a print, it will work best if motifs are closely-spaced. Then select a fabric for the background—don't feel obligated to use beige—and, finally, three or four accent colors, which can also be prints, as long as they co-ordinate with the main fabric. Be sure you have a variety of tones and textures in the color and print designs of your final fabric selection. If you study the fabric swatches and feel that the assortment needs some life, don't be afraid to use more colors.

The photographs of the finished quilts on pages 74 - 94 will surely provide you with inspiration, and they will afford you an opportunity to study at length a variety of color plans, evaluating what you like about each one, or what want to change. You might also study the religious meanings of various colors (see pages 7)for a suggestion for a color plan. If you are planning to make a piece for a specific season of the church year, you will want to pay particular attention to the liturgical colors for that season.

Yardage Estimates

The amounts of fabric suggested below are more than sufficient to make a full-size (56" X 72") quilt with all twelve of the 8" blocks, including a 9"-wide border, like "Precious Memories" on page 74. The amounts of fabrics suggested will allow for some errors.

If you want to make a larger quilt, it is easy to add additional borders; you must, of course, have additional fabrics.

Main fabric: 2 yards

Accent fabrics: ⅓ yard of each color/print you select

Background: 3½ yards, which allows for a 9" border that will give a nice width on which to place an appliquéd motif. Cut borders from the lengthwise of fabric along one side to avoid piecing.

Setting Blocks (Alternate Blocks) (if different from background): 3 yards, which allows sufficient for a 3" wide outside border.

Backing: 5 yards

Templates

When this book was originally written, ten years ago, no one had any idea how to make a quilt other than by using pattern pieces. Some people still like to work this way, and so pattern pieces are included for each of the Bible blocks. (The current method for cutting geometric patchwork—strip-cutting with a rotary cutter—is also included for each block where applicable.)

If you are going to use pattern pieces, you must first make a template of sturdy material for each of the shapes used in the design. Trace the pattern from the book onto a piece of template material, using a fine-line pen or pencil. Cut the template out with paper scissors, not your fabric scissors. (All templates (except applique) in this book already contain ¼" seam allowances.)

When you have cut out your template, punch a hole at seam intersections with a ⅛" hole puncher (available at stationery stores).

Place the template on the wrong side of the fabric, being aware of grain line, and trace around the template. Mark seam intersections with a dot.

Remove template, and use a ruler (or French curve) to draw lines between the dots. These are your seamlines.

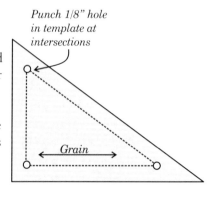

Punch 1/8" hole in template at intersections

Grain

Trace the template as many times as needed to obtain the number of pieces required for each block. When pieces are cut, be sure to place all the shapes needed for one block together in a plastic bag with a closure.

Use good scissors (or rotary cutter) to cut your fabric.

Repeat this procedure for each shape required to make the design; if the shape must be cut in more than one fabric, do not forget to cut it in all the fabrics and in the quantity you need for each block.

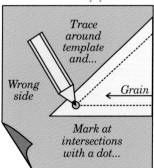

Trace around template and...

Wrong side

Grain

Mark at intersections with a dot...

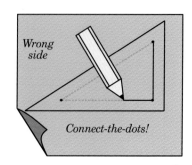

Wrong side

Connect-the-dots!

Construction Hints & Tips

Rotary Cutting Tips - *The Gospel According to Kaye: Chapter 1*

Rotary cutters first came on the market in the early 1980s, and from the first time I used one, I was convinced that the speed and accuracy afforded by this tool would revolutionize quiltmaking. It has - the beauty of using this tool is that you can eliminate that step of marking the fabric. You just have to check and make sure that you always have a ¼" seam allowance included on all sides of the piece, then start cutting. One word of caution, though: the cutter demands your respect, because it is very sharp. Always close the cutter guard when you lay the cutter down, even for a second - it's much easier to snap the guard open than it is to treat a nasty cut to yourself or someone else.

I prefer to make my first cut on a piece of fabric with the fold facing toward me, and I disregard the selvage edges - I just use the factory fold as my straight-edge. I know some home economics teachers are fainting when I say this, but let's face it - most fabrics today are not printed on-grain, so why get up tight over whether or not the fabric is on grain?

If my first cut is to be 3" wide, I will cut it a little wider than I need, then turn it over and clean it up to make a 3" strip. All successive cuts can be made knowing you are dealing with a 90-degree angle. This avoids those nasty bumps on your strips—most of you know about this! At this point, I fold my fabric up again, making for a shorter stroke to cut, and believe it or not, this saves your arms and shoulders some wear.

The small rulers are easier for me to use for all my cross-cuts, and I rely on the large squares for truing up corners and cutting larger blocks.

Rotary-cutting half-squares and quarter-square triangles

The traditional method for cutting half-square triangles requires you to know the finished size of the short sides (the short sides will be the same length), and to this measurement you add ⅞". Cut a square of this size, then cut on the diagonal to make two triangles of the required size.

This is the method you use to cut the corner squares in a quilt set on the diagonal.

In the quarter-square triangle, the short sides will turn out to be on the bias, and the long side will be on the straight of grain. To draw the square, you will need to know the required size of the long leg of the finished triangle, and add 1¼" to that measurement. Draw your square to that size. Cross-cut the square diagonally from corner to corner to yield four quarter-square triangles.

Use this method to cut the side triangles for a quilt set on the diagonal.

Hand or Machine Piecing? - *The Gospel According to Kaye: Chapter 2*

Your decision whether to piece by hand or machine will depend entirely on how your life is going at the time you get ready to put the quilt together. Hand piecing is certainly relaxing, and it is very mobile—I haven't seen a sewing machine on the Little League field or in the doctor's office, but I've seen hand piecers in both places. You make the choice.

Most of the blocks will piece very well on the machine. If you are experienced, everything can be done this way. However, I believe that many people who make a "Journey to Jericho" quilt will want to hand-piece it, especially if the quilt is part of a Bible study class. So, for you hand-piecers, here are some points I think you should keep in mind to make the work go smoothly.

First make sure you have all your supplies on hand, including needles, fine pins, scissors and thread to match your fabric. It's best to use 100 percent cotton thread with 100 percent cotton fabric. Never cut your thread longer than 18", as it tends to knot and tangle. A small needle (like a size 10-12 "between") will help you get more stitches to the inch.

Determine the sequence of assembly ahead of time. It is very useful to work on a fleece board (foam core covered with fleece); you can lay out all the pieces for one block, then stand back and admire your color choices. If something doesn't quite suit you, this is the time to change it.

The piecing diagram and instructions that accompany each block will tell you the best sequence for sewing the pieces together. Study them to determine where to begin.

Choose the first two pieces to be joined and put them right sides together. Pin at each end, where the pencil lines meet, and once in the middle. (Most right-handed people will generally sew right to left and lefties will go

Construction Hints & Tips

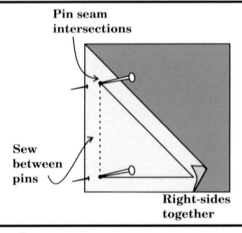

Pin seam intersections

Sew between pins

Right-sides together

left to right. Your stitch will be the same.) Start by taking a small back stitch, and then make your running stitches across the seamline. Occasionally, take a back stitch to strengthen the seam. Lock the seam at the end with another backstitch. Try for at least 10 stitches per inch.

Setting In

If you have to set a piece into a section (A), place the piece to be set in right sides together with the section (B). Line up seams, pin and sew between seam intersections. Press

open. Fold over unsewn seam, align seams, pin intersections, and sew (C). Press open (D).

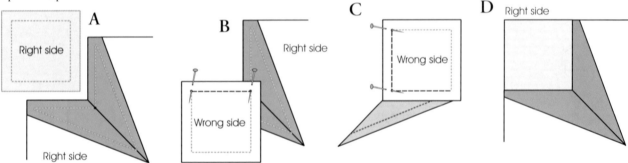

Needle-turn Appliqué

Successful appliqué begins with the cutting and marking of the shape; the seamline is marked on the right side of the fabric. Because the sewing line visible, you know exactly where to turn the seam allowances under.

I use a #11 sharp needle and thread to match the piece. Turn the seam allowance to the wrong side of the piece being appliquéd

(called the appliqué from this point on). Bring the needle up and through the base fabric, plus the seam allowance of the appliqué, then through the fold of the appliqué.

To make a stitch, pass the needle back down slightly ahead of the previous stitch; try for small stitches no more than ⅛" long.

Turn the seam allowance of the appliqué under with the tip of the needle as you move around the shape.

Cutting the Setting (Alternate) Blocks, Outside and Corner Triangles

If you look closely at the finished quilts in this book, you will find that many of the pieced blocks have a narrow border (sashing) around them. This border can be of any width; it will, however, determine the size of the setting blocks.

After the borders are applied to all four sides of the patterned block, measure length and width from raw edge to raw edge. The setting blocks will be cut to this size.

For the outside triangles, see the directions for rotary-cutting quarter-square triangles on page 68. For the corner triangles, see the directions for rotary-cutting half-square triangles on previous page.

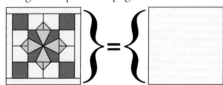

Construction Hints & Tips

Making the diagonal set

To put the quilt together in a diagonal set, consult your setting plan to determine where the "Bible" blocks and the setting blocks should go. Sew them together, one below the other, until the row is complete. Cap each row end with an outside triangle or corner triangle as the setting diagram indicates. Sew the finished rows together.

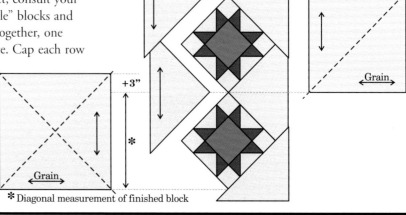

* Diagonal measurement of finished block

Applying Borders

There are two types of borders, square-end and mitered. Square-ends are somewhat quicker to apply, but mitered borders are more appropriate if you will be appliquéing in the border.

Square-end borders are applied by attaching same-size strips first to two opposite sides of the quilt, next to the two remaining sides. The width of the strips is up to you, but their length is determined by measuring up-and-down the quilt at its center. Sew the first pair of border strips to the sides of the quilt. Next, measure across the quilt, through the center, including the border, and cut the strips for the top and bottom borders to this length.

Repeat this procedure for each border you put on the quilt. We live in a time when multiple borders are all the rage, so you may need to repeat these steps three or four times.

To make a mitered border, measure the strips as directed above, add extra length to equal two border widths plus a ¼" seam allowance. Center the border strips on all sides of the quilt top, with excess fabric equally divided between the ends. Stitch all four borders to the quilt top. Leaving excess length free.

To make the miter, fold the quilt top, right sides together, so that two adjoining sides are aligned and 45° angle is formed by the fold and extends into the borders to be mitered. Sew along the line of the extended 45° angle. Trim away excess fabric to ¼" and press seam allowances open.

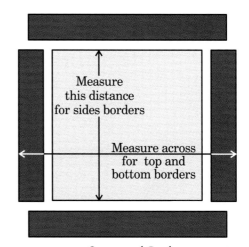

Square-end Borders

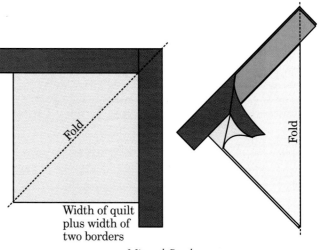

Mitered Borders

Construction Hints & Tips

Using Bias to Make Vines - *The Gospel According to Kaye: Chapter 3*

This method is very quick and almost foolproof. It doesn't matter if your seam allowance varies, as vines are different widths and it gives your quilt a realistic look. Study your quilt, with its borders sewn in place, to determine how you wish your vine to flow. I recommend marking the final movement lightly with pencil.

Choose the fabric you want to use for your vine(s). Cut bias strips 1½" wide, in lengths approximately the same as the different segments of vine. The vine does not need to pass underneath other appliquéd designs; it just needs to look like it does.

Fold the bias strip in half, wrong sides together. Place it on your sketched pencil line, pinning in place if you need to, and being careful on sharp curves not to stretch the bias. Machine-stitch ¼" from the raw edges. When all vines have been machine-stitched in place, fold the strip over to enclose the raw edges, and hand or machine-stitch the vine to the background along the fold.

If my design calls for leaves, I just cut them free-hand. Any shape and size looks great on this type of quilt. If you are not comfortable doing this, refer to books or use the shapes we have given you in the appliqué pattern section. Most importantly, let the design be part of your planning and make it uniquely yours.

Pressing - **The Gospel According to Kaye: Chapter 4**

To steam or not to steam, that is the question. I say steam if you want weird shaped pieces, otherwise don't steam. Steam is like a vice we have—used in moderation it's okay, but overused it is deadly. Most people iron as if they were really mad at the fabric and therefore can completely change the shape without realizing it. A dry iron has less chance to distort your piecing, especially if working with bias edges. Remember to let the iron glide by itself and not to ride on it. It's real easy with steam. If you prefer working with steam, by all means do so. Just be careful and be aware of the dangers. When pressing appliqué. I prefer to press face down in a towel and then I use steam, but not to excess.

Making the Quilt Sandwich - **The Gospel According to Kaye: Chapter 5**

I have this little thing with myself, that if I choose my backing fabrics out of my stash, it somehow makes me feel good about my stashing habits. I really like backs that use more than one fabric, and I don't mind at all adding a piece to the sides or top to make it fit. Some quilts today have great backs, which adds to the interest of the quilt, so stay loose about choosing the fabric for your backs and even try to use some of your leftovers. Then you can rush out and buy more to replace that yardage! Let's face it, a quilt requires lots of work, so why not make the back as neat-looking as the front?

To sandwich your quilt, lay the prepared backing out on a flat surface. (For my backing, I choose to sew strips on each side of the larger piece. This way, I have two seams down the back, rather than one down the center.) Have a friend help you smooth the quilt back and then, using masking tape, tape the back in position. Place batt on back and then add the quilt top. Make sure your back and batt are larger than the top.

Working from the center out, baste all three layers together. You may use large running stitches for this. Baste from the center to one side, then from the center to the opposite side. Then baste from the center to the top and from the center to the bottom. Then follow this technique for basting to the corners. If necessary, put basting stitches between these, always radiating out in one direction, then the opposite direction.

When basting from one side of the quilt to the opposite side, I start with a long thread, baste to one side, leaving enough thread at the center to re-thread my needle and baste to the opposite side. An alternative approach is to always start at the center with a backstitch and baste outward.

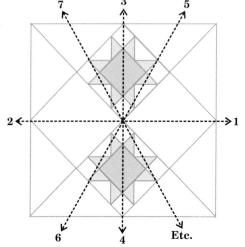

Construction Hints & Tips

Quilting by Hand - *The Gospel According to Kaye, Chapter 6*

Quilting will finish your quilt by adding depth and dimension. Quilting is simply a plain old running stitch, except you're making it through three layers instead of one. I really feel you should try to quilt with nothing larger than a size 10 "between" needle. If you use a large needle it becomes more difficult to achieve tiny, even stitches. You should practice keeping your stitches even, top and bottom—it's better to make large, even stitches than small, uneven ones. As in most things, if you have a plan that works for you, then stay with it.

When hand-quilting, use a short length of thread, no longer than 18". My preference is to avoid knotting the thread end, because I feel this way: if you can pop the knot through the backing to get started, then sometime during the quilt's life, that knot will pop back out. Instead, I float the needle and backstitch before quilting, then backstitch and float when I end a thread.

To float the needle, start by inserting the length of the needle through the top into the batt (not through the back!). Bring the needle out until only the eye is still inside the quilt. Turn the needle point back away from the direction of quilting, and, with your thimble, push the eye end of the needle forward in the batt another length of the needle. Bring the needle back out, eye first, but not all the way. You will have floated the needle two needle lengths and may continue in this way, or, if starting a thread, you may backstitch and begin. I prefer to have approximately 3" of thread floating at the start and end of a quilting thread. This will leave the tail in between the layers and you can hardly pull this out. Before I backstitch at the beginning of a thread I pull the loose end into the quilt. After backstitching and floating the needle at the end of the thread, I pull it taut and cut it, forcing the thread to pull back into the quilt.

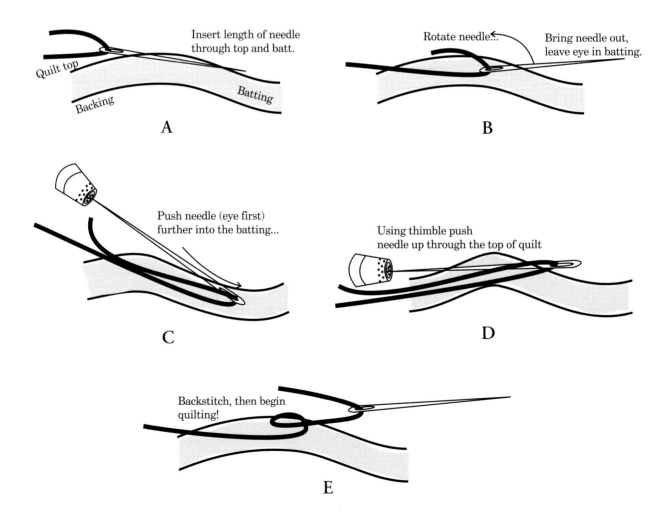

A — Insert length of needle through top and batt. Quilt top / Backing / Batting

B — Rotate needle. Bring needle out, leave eye in batting.

C — Push needle (eye first) further into the batting...

D — Using thimble push needle up through the top of quilt

E — Backstitch, then begin quilting!

Construction Hints & Tips

Quilting by Machine - *The Gospel According to Kaye: Chapter 7*

While I recognize that many quilters still believe that the only quilting acceptable is hand quilting, I encourage you to just give machine quilting a chance! Because it goes so much faster than traditional hand quilting, it offers a greater opportunity to give your loved ones quilts during your lifetime, and I believe it requires as much talent to be a great machine quilter as it does to be a great hand quilter.

I will not debate which method has the greatest value, as I believe it is in the eyes of the beholder. I like both methods, believe both methods have their place, and happily use both methods. My favorite analogy on this subject is this: Few of you are still pounding clothes on a rock in a stream to wash them, so relax and think about another way of quilting! Give it a try.

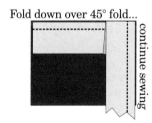

Applying the Binding

When quilting is finished, all that is left to do is apply a binding to the four outer raw edges. Many people really enjoy this step, because it means they're just about through with another quilt.

Choose binding fabric with careful thought. It is a design element of the quilt top, although it's just a narrow strip on the very outer edge. We've all had the experience of seeing an old quilt that has been re-bound with a careless choice of color or print, so we know how jarring it can be, plus it makes you feel sorry for the poor quilt. Bear in mind that the edges of a quilt which will be used will get lots of wear, and pick a color or print that doesn't show dirty fingerprints, if possible.

Cut bias strips of fabric 2½" wide. Cut bindings on the bias only if it is necessary to do so—for example, to make a stripe go a certain way.

Fold in half wrong sides together (don't press), and place along edge of quilt top, raw edges aligned. Beginning in the middle of one side of the quilt, machine-stitch in place with a ¼" seam.

To turn the binding at a corner, stop stitching within ¼" of the end; clip threads. Slip work from beneath presser foot and fold binding up (see illustration), making a 45-degree angle, then fold back down so the edges on the next side to be sewn are aligned and the last fold is aligned with the edge just stitched. Slip work back under the needle, positioning it ¼" in from both edges, lower the presser foot and continue stitching to the next corner, where you will repeat these steps until all four corners have been rounded.

Fold the binding over the seam to the back of the quilt and whip-stitch into place.

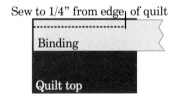

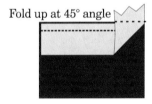

Fabric Care - *The Gospel According to Kaye: Chapter 8*

We could discuss this subject for months and months and still not agree on the final results. I do not wash my fabric before use, but I do test for colorfastness. This is such an important topic, I prefer to tell you what I do and then have you make your own choices. As in all things, you must do what works for you, but I just can't make myself wash fabric that isn't dirty!

The Quilts and Their Stories

From the beginning, this book has inspired and helped to heal many individuals. Numerous quilters have reported working through grief over the loss of a loved one, or through worry while a family member faced a critical health issue, by making a "Journey to Jericho" quilt. As the book found its way across the country, it was adopted as a lesson guide for Sunday school classes and Women of the Church groups.

Precious Memories
Kaye England
56" X 72"

"The quilt's name is the same as that of a hymn by J.B.F. Wright. One line goes, 'As I travel on life's pathway, I know not what the years may hold.' So true, but we are ever eager to make the journey.

"'As I ponder, hope grows fonder, precious memories flood my soul.' I take great comfort in these lines and as I stitched the vines and leaves in the border I was reminded that hope abounds for all who believe, and I was pleasantly consumed by all my thoughts.

"I chose strong bright colors to represent my belief that we all can be stars in this life and hereafter. Also, I believe Daddy and my brother Rex will like this."

Kaye's Quilts

Kaye England has experienced the same emotions as many of the other quilters who have turned to a combination of their religious faith and their love of quilting in times of grief, sorrow, and/or transition. She quilted while she nursed her mother through breast cancer, and kept on quilting after her mother lost her fight with the disease. She made quilts in memory of her beloved father and brother, both of whom she lost too early in life. And finally, she made a quilt to commemorate her 41-year marriage to her husband, who died suddenly during the first year of this new century. Again and again, Kaye has made memorials to those in her family who have preceded her to the Great Beyond.

On the other hand, Kaye has made quilts to celebrate happy occasions in her life. Much of her work speaks to the joy she takes in her friends, family and her work. Here, then, is a presentation of the quilts Kaye has been inspired to make from the patterns in this book, accompanied by her commentary on each quilt.

Friendship Sampler
65" X 65"
Some of my favorite things are represented on this quilt. The hand is for friendship; the butterfly is for resurrection; a pineapple represents, as it has since Colonial times, hospitality; a pomegranate is for the amazing fertility of life (who would have guessed I'd have six wonderful grandchildren?); and various flowers for the abundance of blessings in our lives. I've always loved the little folk-art angel, and what better place to use her than on a Bible-inspired quilt?

The Ladder and the Star
52" x 60"

I designed this quilt as a tribute to my married life. "Bethlehem Star" represents the light that guided David and me through our many years together, and the "Jacob's Ladder" is for the many obstacles one must overcome to make a marriage endure. The leaves represent the 41 years we were together, and the two large flowers are for our two children. I believe David will be waiting at the top of the ladder for me.

This poem came to me on a plane about a year after David's unexpected death. I'd been thinking about the quilt I had just finished, and these lines flowed from my pen:

The Ladder and the Star

As I pieced Jacob's Ladder and Bethlehem Star
I thought of their meanings in my life, so far.

The Ladder is the joys and blessings I've been given,
The Star's soft glimmer is a message from heaven.

The Ladder represents our journey as mates
The Star says that God is in charge of our fates.

The Ladder—alone I've many rungs yet to climb,
The Star—will guide, comfort, and give peace of mind.

The Ladder tells me to always stay a dreamer
The Star tells me I'll find rest with my Redeemer.

Purple Majesty
37" X 37"

"'Job's Tears' is a favorite block of mine, so I elected to use it in this piece. I chose the colors to be symbolic of his life: green because it represents the triumph of life over death, and purple for its secondary meaning of sorrow and penitence. I felt the addition of the butterflies were a sign of Job's re-birth and his continued trust in God, even through many trials."

Joseph's "Confetti" Coat
36" X 36"

"A new fabric line was the perfect inspiration for this wallhanging. and it was a natural for this block. We can only imagine the beauty of that great "garment of love" given to Joseph by his aged father."

Evening Stars for Joseph
37" X 37".

"Here's another color variation of the "Joseph's Coat" block, using stars as background. I imagined this brightly colored coat against an evening sky full of color, and I was happy."

Kaye's Quilts

Butterflies are Free

36" X 36".

"The 'Star of Bethlehem' is symbolic of the birth of Jesus and a world forever changed by that event. I used gray as a dominant color because it symbolizes the death of the body and the immortality of the spirit. The butterflies ('free' because they are printed on the fabric!) represent His triumphant return."

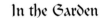

In the Garden

36" X 36"

"There's another old hymn that's a favorite of mine, which begins, 'I come to the garden alone, while the dew is still on the roses.' It came to mind as I finished this wallhanging and began thinking of the different quilt blocks named after roses and other flowers. Then I thought about how the growth of the spirit is the same as the growth of the flowers, in that both are in constant need of care if they are to flourish. The chorus of the hymn goes, 'And He walks with me, and He talks with me, and He tells me I am His own. . . .' As I remembered these lines, I was reminded that we do not come to the garden alone."

In the Beginning

36" X 36"

"Nothing is more representative of the 'Beginning' to me as the 'Tree of Life.' It signifies the beginning of all mankind—full of faults and full of hope. I also see the tree as a symbol of family life. The use of green symbolizes the triumph of spring over winter, of life over death. I originally dedicated this project to my mother in the hope that she would find new hope and be triumphant in her recovery."

Jacob's Journey

48" X 48"

"A collection of hand-dyed solids combined with black and cocoa brown were the start of this project. As I worked, I thought of how Jacob certainly had a long journey, and so I decided to use the different colors of blocks to represent different stages of his life. Black is for his sickness; green is for the regeneration of his soul through good works; purple is a sign of earned power; red for emotions; gold for divinity; and brown symbolizes the years he spent in service to God."

I t's interesting to observe that several of the quilts presented on the pages that follow were the first quilts ever made by many of the women. Must have been the Spirit at work! Although many of Kaye's friends have quilted to find peace while enduring stressful situations, an equal or greater number have made quilts to celebrate the presence of God in their lives.

Note: Direct quotes are the quiltmaker's own statements about their work.

Heirs of the Promise
Lois D. Griffin

Formerly of Terre Haute, Indiana now of Cave Creek, Arizona
59½" X 63½"

"This quilt depicts traditional quilt blocks based on Bible themes, and was designed in conjunction with the book *Journey to Jericho* (first edition), by Kaye England. The vine and branches are the design of the quiltmaker.

"Throughout the quilting history of America, these blocks have helped quilters tell Bible stories from Genesis to Revelation, from Adam to Christ."

In addition to the twelve blocks featured in the book, Lois devised a "Doves" block that makes unique use of the traditional "Rob Peter to Pay Paul" quilt design. Four blocks of the basic design are made of white and a dark print, then set together to form the doves.

Journey to Jericho
Elizabeth Gay Nordvik

Fort Wayne, Indiana
71¼" X 86½"

"My quilt was pieced and quilted during a Bible study at the Covenant United Methodist Church in Fort Wayne," reports Elizabeth. She worked with eight-inch square blocks which she border with a ¾" white strip, to equal a finished square of 9½". The patterned blocks alternate in a diagonal set with dark green mossy print squares, each of which Elizabeth quilted with a feathered wreath.

The geometric borders of this quilt give it a distinctive appearance. The first border, around the field of the quilt, is a ⅝" wide strip of print fabric. The second border, 6½" wide, consists of three very elongated triangles for each side, which were mathematically designed, according the Elizabeth. The third border is another ⅝" wide print strip, and the fourth is made of "Fancy Nine-Patch" squares set on the diagonal. The fifth border is a 4" wide brown on tan strip, quilted with a cable design.

Kaye's Friends' Quilts

My Journey
Lisa Cart

Jonesboro, Indiana
82½" X 98½" (quilt top)

"I loved the idea of making a quilt with blocks that had Bible-related names. As the years go by, I appreciate more and more the gifts of God's creation, such as beautiful flowers, graceful butterflies, and fascinating hummingbirds. Rainbows remind me of God's incredible plan of salvation, and also how grateful I am for the opportunity to have fellowship with Him.

"I looked for a main fabric that had purple, green, and gold, then chose the other fabrics after that. The background and border fabrics, along with the appliquéd flowers, remind me of my own little 'Garden of Eden' in my back yard.

"I enjoy comparing my quilt with the one my aunt, Esther Russell, made. It's a lesson to me that, although our two quilts are made from the same pattern, they are so different—just like people!

"God has blessed me with two daughters, Bethany and Amber. I plan to make another version of this quilt, so that I may pass on to each of them a quilt made with love. God is good!"

The Good News
Esther Russell

Muncie, Indiana

"I used a background that I imagine to be the color of the land of the Bible, because I've always loved the story of how the early believers would signal their faith to one another by drawing a fish in the sand with their toe. That story was also, of course, the inspiration for the first border.

"The outer border is inspired by **John 15:1**, which says "*I am the true vine, and my Father is the gardener.*" A grape leaf from my yard served as the pattern for my appliquéd leaves.

"When I made the 'Hosanna' block, I though about what a joy it would have been to be in that cheering crowd that greeted Jesus on his entry into Jerusalem, and waving palm branches along with them.

"Working on this quilt gave me a chance to have sweet fellowship with a niece, Lisa Cart, who is making one too."

Joseph's Coat
Mary Elizabeth Johnson

Montgomery, Alabama
Quilted by Terry Owens, Huntsville, Alabama
73" X 89"

"When Kaye asked me to work with her on the revision of *Journey to Jericho,* and when we decided that we'd definitely want to include some new quilts in the revised book, I wanted one of those new quilts to be mine!

"I decided that I wanted to make a full-size quilt with a repeat block design, rather than a sampler of each of the twelve designs.

"I pulled my fabrics, beginning with a pomegranate design because pomegranates are mentioned so often in the Bible, and, when I was a child in south Alabama, we'd had a pomegranate tree growing in our back yard.

I liked the star at the center of each "Joseph's Coat" block. It was, however, a surprise to see the star disappear when the blocks were set together. That's why I made the stars for the corners of one of the borders.

"I love Terry's machine quilting designs and the fact that she used four different threads, one of which is a gold metallic, to quilt the piece."

Kaye's Friends' Quilts

Journey to Jericho
Quilters of the Carmel United Methodist Church

Carmel, Indiana
88" X 108"

A framed plaque, which hangs beneath the quilt in the church, contains the following description of the piece:

"This quilt, which was made by the quilters of Carmel United Methodist Church, is based on Kaye England's book, Journey to Jericho," with the title inspired by the parable of the Good Samaritan. **Luke 10:29-37.**

"There are twelve blocks, representing the twelve apostles. Six alternate blocks symbolize divine power, majesty, wisdom, love, mercy, and justice. Ten side blocks are the number of the Commandments. Four corner blocks stand for the four Gospels. The number three for the Trinity is shown in the *fleur-de-lis* quilted in the corner blocks. Eternity is represented in the quilt's construction - the top is the beginning, the batting is the middle, and the backing is the end. The layers are all stitched together with the same thread."

A separate panel in the plaque gives the Bible verse that is the inspiration for each of the blocks, as well as a list of the colors used in the quilt and what each color represents.

Journey to Jericho
Connie Molz

Kokomo, Indiana
49½" X 50"

"This quilt was therapy for me after my mother died of breast cancer. The silver lamé square in the center represents the bright white light she saw just before God called her to heaven," wrote Connie.

The colors Connie chose for her quilt, in addition to the very significant silver lamé, are drawn from the one print she used. She pulled a purple, three pinks, a green and a turquoise from the print to use in piecing the nine blocks of her quilt. Each of her eight-inch blocks is enlarged to 9½" by the addition of a white border, and the quilt is finished with a white border into which Connie quilted a feathered cable.

Amen
Gail Curnutt

Arlington, Texas
34" X 34"

"My inspiration for this quilt came one morning at dawn, as I watched the sun light up the snow that lay on the land of the Texas panhandle farm on which I live. The sight was so beautiful that it brought forth a spiritual response from me—this quilt is the result.

"I used the 'World Without End' block because I wanted to be able to create circles with my color choices. Circles are very meaningful in the literature of the Bible."

Gail's is one of those quilts in which color has been used to create intriguing optical illusions. It is actually built of sixteen "World Without End" blocks. She suggests that you draw the sixteen blocks out on graph paper (and the borders, too, for maximum accuracy), take your chart to a copier and run off a dozen or more, then play with your colored pencils, crayons, or markers until you get a look you like by coloring in the different squares and triangles of the design. Use your colored graph as a guide to pulling fabrics for the quilt.

Journey to Jericho
Kathleen McKenna

Quilted by Debbie Oliver
both of Carmel, Indiana
69½" X 83"

"At the time I decided to take the 'Journey to Jericho' class, I was going through many emotional problems, both in my personal life and at work. In February of that year, I lost my father to cancer. This quilt is dedicated to my father, and some of the fabric was picked out to honor him. For example, my father made a dove out of stained glass which he gave to his church just before he died; I thought of him when I found the white material printed with golden doves.

"The purple fabric signifies both sorrow and royalty. It represents my sorrow at losing my father, but also that he was a 'king among men,' in that he would do anything he could to help someone in need."

Each of the gold setting blocks is beautifully machine-quilted with a different design from *Journey to Jericho*, and the white border is quilted with a passion-flower vine in gold thread. The rich print of the border fabric provides the color palette for the pieced blocks.

Journey to Jericho

Peace
Marti Louk

Carmel, Indiana
63" X 74".

"I knew from the start the quilt would be for my son, Greg. What I didn't know was that the quilt would be for me too! What great therapy it was to work on this quilt after my mother died. I worked my way through all kinds of thoughts and feelings and had some great conversations with God, and by the time the binding went on, I felt I had regained some of the peace that had been missing in my life."

Alice's Refuge
Alice Cunningham

Carmel, Indiana
65" X 77"

"It is difficult to express in words what my 'Bible Quilt' means to me—I have certainly been inspired. The first class literally brought tears to my eyes—calling up the same feelings I had as a small child hearing the truly wondrous stories of the Bible.

"The name of my quilt is taken from **Psalm 46:1**: *'For God is our refuge and strength, a very present help in trouble.'* Quilting can be a haven during times of stress in our lives."

Inspiration
Ursula Zimmerman

Noblesville, Indiana
Quilted by Cecelia Purciful
65" X 77"

"I chose to use the quilting designs for appliqué so that I could incorporate the plants from the Holy Land in the border.

"I have been strip piecing for a few years and have made several quilts and wallhangings but when Kaye England and Quilt Quarters offered a class in Bible quilts, I was certain it was a perfect gift for my daughter-in-law."

My Garden of Eden
Excelda W. Shaw
West Lafayette, Indiana
52" X 66"

"The color green is used in this quilt to symbolize the plants in the Garden of Eden. I chose yellow for the alternate blocks because yellow reminds me of the sun in the Garden and the Son who gives us light. It also provided the perfect background for quilting the plants of the Bible, which I wanted in my Garden. In the center of my Garden, I placed the 'Tree of Life,' just as God did in Eden."

Genesis
Joanie Rohn
Danville, Indiana
30" X 30"

"I have always been drawn to the 'Storm at Sea' design, possibly because I could see a correlation between the constant motion in the quilt and the seemingly constant chaos in my life. As I faced my 40th birthday, I decided to 'calm the seas' and so have added the 'Mariner's Compass' to guide me in beginning this new and exciting journey."

In the Vine
Excelda W. Shaw

West Lafayette, Indiana
72" X 86"

"The colors I chose for this quilt —reds, blues, purples, and lavender—symbolize love, truth, royalty and power. I wanted a stained glass effect because I love the stained glass windows of churches. The vine in the border symbolizes our new relationship to God from the cross (bottom) to the lamb (top) who sits upon the throne. The dove is a symbol of our baptism."

Inspiration
Caryl Schuetz

Indianapolis, Indiana
36" X 36"

"I made this quilt to look like an 1890's piece, deliberately seeking fabrics and colors similar to those used in quilts of that time—dark blues, browns and tans, plaids and stripes. I have been studying and collecting quilts from the 1800s for years, and as a result, some of my work has been influenced by the styles of that century. Another reason I chose the 'old' look was because the Bible was a popular influence during the 1800s.

"The butterflies were selected as much for their symbolism as for their beauty. To me, my quilt is inspirational, a symbol of my hope and faith."

On the Road from Jerusalem to Jericho
Lucille Garrett

Crawfordsville, Indiana
Quilted by Cecelia Purciful
52" X 64"

"I really liked learning about the Christian symbols and the meanings of the colors. My favorite colors in this quilt are green and purple, denoting new life, royalty and power. I have numerous unfinished tops and this is the first quilt I have completed. I shall cherish this quilt forever. It has introduced me to a new aspect in quilting."

On Eagles' Wings
Teresa Gunn

Indianapolis, Indiana
52" X 52"

"The name comes from a line in one of my favorite hymns, which is based on **Psalm 91**. Whenever I sing that hymn, a special feeling comes over me, and I am reminded of God's protection. I started my quilt during Lent, and the colors I chose reflect this season of rebirth. I believe the only way to improve my quilting or anything in my life is to 'stretch my wings and soar.'"

Back of Quilt

Entwined In Vines
Connie Clark

Sheridan, Indiana
60" X 72"

"**Ecclesiastes 3:1** says, '*To everything there is a season, and a time to every purpose.*' This quilt is dedicated to the memory of Cecil Bennett, a lovely lady who lived 96 years and told charming stories of growing up in a German Catholic home."

Glory in Bethlehem
Debra Danko

Greenfield, Indiana
Quilted by Cecelia Purciful
65" X 77"

"This is the first full-size quilt I have completed, and it reflects my interests. I enjoyed sharing the blocks with my friends and family as I progressed."

Kaye's Friends' Quilts

Searching for Life
Paula Guffy

Carmel, Indiana
36" X 76"

"I feel that the four blocks I chose for my quilt were telling me that searching is what life is all about. It is searching for heaven, for growth, for a better life, and for eternal life. The vine going around the quilt symbolizes God, who surrounds us, and who is always there when we need Him and is waiting for us to accept Him. The butterflies are a sign of the resurrection that tell us, with our faith in God, we can have eternal life."

The Beauty of the Creation
Kathleen Springer

Westfield, Indiana
42" X 42"

"The print used in the border was the inspiration for my quilt. I wanted to do something that reflected the natural beauty of the earth, so I chose solid chintz to complement the elegance of the print. The three blocks used were 'Tree of Life,' 'Storm at Sea,' and 'World Without End.'"

Arbor Day
Danita Rafalovich

Los Angeles, California
36" X 36"

"The 'Tree of Life' block was an easy choice for me because of my botanical education. The 'Crown of Thorns' wreath as the center block was chosen strictly for the graphics. Southern California has a subtle change of seasons and those gentle changes are represented in the four different tree color combinations, thus reminding me of Arbor Day."

Serenity
Geneva Carroll

Carmel, Indiana
42" X 57"

"'The Serenity Prayer' has not only seen me through some tough times, but has taught me a lot. I am thankful for the simple, but powerful words in this prayer.

"The two flower bouquets I quilted into this quilt are reminiscent of my mother's, grandmother's, and great-grandmother's love affairs with flowers. My version of God, placed in the top left corner, is watching over all. In the midst of a hectic life, working on this quilt brought me a sense of peace and tranquility."

Kaye's Friends' Quilts

Favorite Things
Janet Scott
Noblesville, Indiana
65" X 77"
"My first finished quilt and my first attempt at appliqué! As I worked on this quilt, I was often reminded of the line from the Sound of Music song, 'These are a few of my favorite things.' From receiving the class as a gift to the last stitch in the binding I felt I was gathering my favorite things into one keepsake."

Samsong
Kathleen Saunders
Cincinnati, Ohio
50" X 50"
"I started this quilt because I felt left out of the fun everyone was having making projects in the Bible quilt class. It is dedicated to my bird, Sam, who used to sit on my sewing machine chirping away while I sewed. He was sick for several weeks while I worked on this quilt and died the day after I completed the quilt top. I quilted golden birds around the 'Tree of Life' block in his memory."

Armstrong, Karen. *The Battle for God.* New York: The Ballentine Publishing Co., 2000, 2001.

Bowker, John. *The Complete Bible Handbook: An Illlustrated Companion.* London: Dorling Kindersley Limited, 1998. New York: DK Publishing, 2001.

Brackman, Barbara. *Encyclopedia of Pieced Quilt Patterns.* Kansas: Prairie Flower Publishing, 1979.

Comay, Joan. *Who's Who in the Old Testament.* Weidenfeld & Nicholson, 1971.

Davis, J.D. *Dictionary of the Bible.* New Jersey: Fleming H. Revell, 1924.

Doty, William G. *Letters in Primitive Christianity.* Pennsylvania: Fortress Press, 1973.

Dreyfus, Henry. *Symbol Sourcebook.* New York: McGraw Hill, 1972.

Ferguson, George. *Signs and Symbols in Christian Art.* New York: Oxford University Press, 1954.

Fox, Sandi. *Wrapped in Glory.* New York: Thames & Hudson, 1990.

Fry, Gladys Marie. *Stitched From the Soul.* New York: Dutton Studio Books, 1990.

Gordon, C. *The World of the Old Testament.* New York: Doubleday, 1953.

Hopkins, Mary Ellen. *The It's Okay If You Sit On My Quilt Book.* Santa Monica, CA: ME Publications, 1989.

Irwin, John Rice. *A People and their Quilts.* W. Chester, PA: Schiffer Publications, 1984.

Judge, Edwin A. *The Social Patterns of Christians in the First Century.* Illinois: Tyndale House, 1960.

Khin, Yvonne M. *Collector's Dictionary of Quilt Names & Patterns.* Washington, D.C.: Acropolis, 1980.

Kinart, Malvina and Janet Crisler. *Loaves & Fishes.* Connecticut: Keats Publishing, 1975.

Lehner, Ernest & Johanna. *Folklore & Symbolism of Flowers, Plants, & Trees.* Tudor Publishing.

Liby, Shirley. *Bible Blocks, Old & New.* Indiana: Graphics Unlimited, 1991.

Mays, James L., ed. *Harper's Bible Commentary.* San Francisco: Harper & Row, Publishers, 1988.

Metzger, Bruce, David Goldstein, and John Ferguson, eds. *Great Events of Bible Times.* New York; Barnes & Noble Books, 1998. (Originally produced by Reprocolor Llovet, SA of Barcelona, Spain; Marshall Editions, Ltd., copyright 1987.)

Orlofsky, Patsy & Myron. *Quilts in America.* New York: McGraw Hill, 1974.

Payne, Suzy and Murwin, Susan. *Creative American Quilting.* New Jersey: Fleming H. Revell, 1983.

Pearlman, Moshe. *In the Footsteps of the Prophets.* New York: Thomas Crowell, 1975.

Potter, Charles Francis. *Is That in the Bible?* Connecticut: Fawcett Publishing, 1962.

Quilt World editors. *Bible Quilt Blocks.* Pennsylvania: House of White Birches, 1984.

Rehmel, Judy. *Patchwork Patterns from Bible Stories.* Minnesota: Augsberg Fortress.

Sienkiewicz, Elly. *Spoken Without a Word.* Washington, D.C.: Turtle Press, 1983.

Squire, Helen. *A Quilters Garden.* New Jersey: Fleming H. Revell, 1987.

Untermyer, Louis. *Plants of the Bible.* New York: Golden Press.

Wallis, Charles. *Holy Holy Land.* New York: Harper & Row, 1969.

Zohary, Michael. *Plants of the Bible.* New York: Cambridge University.

Other Books by the Authors

By Kaye England:

Voices of the Past

Voices of the Past, Volume II

Callie Lu's Sunflowers

Winter Wonderland

A Civil War Legacy

Vintage Gathering

Somewhere in Time

Double Dozen

With Mary Elizabeth Johnson

Quilt Inspirations from Africa